Favorite Recipes from
America's Bed and Breakfast Inns

Gail Greco

On the cover: Breakfast at the Village Victorian Inn at Rhinebeck, NY.
Photo by George Gardner

On the back cover: Photo of Gail Greco by Tom Bagley. Photo of innkeepers Marsha and Rich Lucidi by Bruce Muncy. Photo of The Queen Victoria, Cape May, N.J. by George Gardner.

A Country Inn Breakfast includes recipes from a variety of American inns. These recipes have been edited and tested by Gail Greco and the American Cooking Guild editors. The inns were selected by the author. No fee was paid by an inn as a provision for being listed.

Edited by Joanne Leonard
Cover and text design by Linda Sherman Design, Inc.
Illustrations for chapter headings by Tom Kozar
Typography by Back Office Support Services

Printed in the United States of America

ISBN 0-942320-40-9

For a catalog of cookbooks write to:
The American Cooking Guild
6-A East Cedar Avenue
Gaithersburg, MD 20877
(301) 963-0698

For mom, who arose even
on the coldest of mornings
to serve us breakfast
from the heart.

Contents

INTRODUCTION

Good Morning, America

We all know that breakfast is the healthy thing to do. In fact, according to experts, skipping the morning meal increases the chance of a heart attack. Apparently, the risk of having a heart attack is greatest in the first few hours after waking, because the daily rhythms of many bodily functions tend to peak then. Aside from the health reasons, though, I just enjoy preparing breakfast on a daily basis and on special occasions for friends. I like to entertain but don't have much time. Breakfast with friends is my answer to getting people together when I'm too busy to do a dinner party.

My husband and I make an effort to take 15 to 20 minutes each morning to share the breakfast table. We usually prepare what we can the night before and we try to make it enticing as an added incentive for getting out of bed. Creative breakfasts will delight your family, too. Most people don't expect interesting dishes for breakfast, so you can be surprising friends and family all the time as you prepare breakfast the way innkeepers do.

Inns offer breakfast in a variety of ways. Some summon guests to the table with the lilt of a bell. Others caddy breakfast to guest rooms or to a patio. In any case, breakfast at inns is a time to savor. "Sometimes, it lasts three hours at our inn," reports Mike Wass of The Whitehall Inn in New Hope, Pennsylvania. Breakfast itself is usually half that time, but Mike and his wife, Suella, often join the guests after the last course is served and the conversation just goes enthusiastically on.

In a time when service with a smile is becoming increasingly rare, it's no wonder that people are attracted to small inns. All across this country, every day of the year, travelers scramble out from under goose-down comforters, roll out of antique beds and climb into clawfoot tubs to begin another day of adventure at a bed-and-breakfast inn. And greeting them downstairs is a smiling innkeeper just waiting to pamper every one.

Bed-and-breakfast (or B&B) and country inns offer a pleasurable lodging alternative and they can also be destinations in themselves. Visiting inns opens new horizons. Under the guidance of your hosts, you can acquire new sports or dancing skills, or gain an increased appreciation of history, music or nature, not to mention, of course, gourmet cooking.

B&Bs differ from country inns. A B&B offers what its name implies—a place to rest and be sent on your way with a full stomach as the sun rises. Country inns may have more guest rooms and offer dinner. However, the term 'country inn' is also used generically to mean any small inn where hospitality to guests is paramount.

The practice of sharing one's home with strangers dates to this nation's founding days. Everyone, from itinerant artisans to horse-mounted politicians and weary tourists stopped at homes that hailed visitors with their folksy signs offering room and breakfast for a few pence. Although England is credited with originating the modern-day bed-and-breakfast concept, it was Americans who nurtured and developed it. In the mid-1980s, many couples, tired of unrewarding corporate jobs, caught the entrepreneurial bug. Thank goodness there was no cure. They bought ramshackle historic homes, saving them from the wrecker's ball and opening them to travelers to enjoy home-away-from-home lodging as never before.

In a true B&B, the innkeeper is always on the premises, or at least very involved in their business. The innkeeper has separate quarters, leaving the entire house for the guests. If the host is merely providing a few spare rooms in his house, it's not really an inn, but rather what we call a homestay.

Country inn breakfasts are an adventure in more than just taste; they are a treat for all the senses. I invite you to use this cookbook to host breakfasts the inn way, but then hit the road and let the innkeepers do the preparing and pampering.

Breakfast Inn Style Menus

When I buy a new cookbook, I rummage through it voraciously, creating menus from the recipes. This makes meal preparations easier and I get more use out of the cookbook. I've done that for you here. A number following an item refers to the page where you will find the recipe. Of course, feel free to add or subtract dishes, or to design your own combinations. Also, tell guests where the recipes came from; talking about inns can spark all kinds of interesting conversation.

Off-To-Work Breakfast

Grapefruit Halves

John Wayne Corn Cheese Casserole, 96

Basil Buttermilk Scones, 68

On The Run

Berry Power Drink, 89

Cinnamon Rolls, 47

Protein Packer

Strawberry Orange Drink, 92

Crab and Pasta Frittata, 99

Broiled Tomatoes au Gratin, 74

Whole-Earth Eye Opener

Apple Paprika Soup, 46

Egyptian Bean Breakfast, 94

❧

Waiting for the School Bus

Cranapple Frappé, 67

Birchermüesli, 44

Peanut Butter Bread, 80

❧

Yippee, it's the Weekend!

Fresh Fruit Cup

Poached Eggs with Lemon Butter Chive Sauce, 19

Redstone Amaretto Coffee, 69

❧

Breakfast for a Visitor

The Governor's Peach Pudding, 24

Plantation Eggs and Beef Casserole, 59

Morning Zucchini Bread, 22

❧

Country Breakfast with Special Friends

Sliced Peaches and Pears

Ham and Cheese Omelet Roll, 26

Mushroom Ragout Timbales, 27

Cinnamon Rolls, 47

❧

Party Time in the A.M.

Chilled Champagne Honeydew Soup, 93

Cardamom French Toast with Red Currant Syrup, 62

Apple Fritters, 21

Redstone Amaretto Coffee, 69

❧

China and Crystal Breakfast

Citrus Mimosa, 70

Lemon Yogurt Poppy Seed Waffles, 37

Poached Pears with Grand Marnier Cream, 50

❧

Teatime Breakfast

Cantaloupe and Honeydew Balls

Ham and Tarragon Eggs in Puff Pastry, 57

Strawberry Bread with Strawberry Cream Cheese , 43

Hot Mint Tea

❧

After-The-Hike Meal

Chilled Champagne Honeydew Soup, 93

Apple and Sausage Stuffed Croissants, 61

Mushroom Ragout Timbales, 27

Orange Marmalade Bread, 81

❧

Exerciser's Breakfast

Cranberry Juice

Orange Oatmeal Pie, 38

Poppy Colada Muffins, 77

❧

Spring Break Breakfast

Citrus Mimosa (non-alcoholic version), 70

Crunchy French Toast with Strawberry Cream Sauce, 102

Butter Coffee Cake, 48

❧

Summer Morning Celebration

The Governor's Peach Pudding, 24

McKay House Orange Pecan Toast, 64

Blueberry Poppy Seed Brunch Cake with Lemon Curd, 45

❧

First Fall Feast

Cranapple Frappé, 67

Cabbage Rose Granola, 36

Apple Butter French Toast, 49

❧

Thanksgiving Day Breakfast

Fresh Fruit Cup Sprinkled with Nuts

Apple Oat Bran Muffins, 75

Cheddar Sandwiches with Maple Cranberry Apricot Sauce, 95

❧

The Colonial Way to Start the Day

Apple Paprika Soup, 46

Rum Cornmeal Johnnycakes, 51

Blueberry Streusel Muffins, 73

❧

On Christmas Morn

Cranapple Frappé, 67

Blushing Rose Featherbed Eggs, 39

Cheese-Filled Poppy Seed Muffins, 91

Apple Dumplings with Spicy Rum Sauce, 42

❧

Winter Warmer

Tangerine Sections

Maple Porridge, 25

Basil Buttermilk Scones, 68

❧

From a Plantation Kitchen

Apple Fritters, 21

Crabmeat Eggs in Creole Hollandaise, 102

Broiled Tomatoes au Gratin, 74

❧

Southern Style

Fresh Peaches

Creamy Hash Browns with Chicken, Mushrooms and Cheese, 58

Honey Run Sticky Buns, 82

❧

New England Riser

Sliced Oranges

Maple Porridge, 25

Apple Pie Pancakes, 55

❧

Tropical Tastes

Hawaiian Müesli, 98

Mango Bread, 20

Pele's Baked Pear Dumplings with Lemon Sauce and Coconut, 97

❧

Bon Jour

Strawberry Orange Drink, 92

Croissants à l'Orange, 23

Poached Pears with Grand Marnier Cream, 50

❧

Scotland Yard at Daybreak

Grapefruit Juice

Sausage and Hash Brown Mini-Frittatas, 56

Popovers with Strawberries Romanoff, 71

❧

Mediterranean Mixer

Red and Green Grapes

Crab and Pasta Frittata, 99

Italian Plum Coffee Cake, 34

Redstone Amaretto Coffee, 69

❧

Ethnic Breakfast Fusion

Strawberries Romanoff, 72

Open-Faced Breakfast Tortillas, 41

Swedish Almond Twists, 84

Recipe Index

Beverages

Fruit Fantasies

Cereals

Reason To Rise: Breads, Rolls, Biscuits, Muffins, Cakes

New England

Manor House

NORFOLK, CONNECTICUT

Diane and Henry Tremblay have the kind of home in which many of us could pursue regal fantasies. Manor House is a stately English country estate set among tall and gracious trees. A baronial cherry-paneled staircase and cross-walk leads to guest rooms decorated in country Victorian.

Poached Eggs with Lemon Butter Chive Sauce

This is an easy way to prepare a gourmet breakfast.

4	eggs
1	tablespoon vinegar
1/3	cup butter
2	tablespoons finely chopped fresh chives
1	tablespoon lemon juice
1/2	teaspoon salt
1/4	teaspoon black pepper
2	English muffins, halved and toasted

Poach the eggs for 3 to 4 minutes in simmering water to which the vinegar has been added.

For the sauce, melt the butter in a small saucepan, add the chives, lemon juice, salt and pepper and beat thoroughly.

When the eggs are just set, remove them from the pan with a slotted spoon and drain on paper towels.

To serve, place a poached egg on a toasted English muffin half and pour sauce over top.

Yield: 2 to 4 servings.

The Cape Neddick House

CAPE NEDDICK, MAINE

This inn is characterized by friendliness, Victorian decor, and strong family ties. The 1880s house has been in the innkeeper's family since it was built. As the Goodwins serve breakfast, they also offer tales of days past and interesting tidbits about the inn's curious architecture and furnishings.

Mango Bread

With mangoes becoming so much easier to find at the market nationwide, I told innkeeper Diane Goodwin we just had to have this very moist bread recipe for another way to use the exotic fruit.

2	eggs
1 1/4	cups sugar
1/2	cup corn or canola oil
1/4	cup honey
2	cups ripe mango, peeled, cut up and slightly mashed
2	cups all-purpose flour
2	teaspoons baking soda
2	teaspoons cinnamon
1/2	teaspoon salt
1/2	teaspoon vanilla extract
1/2	cup chopped walnuts
1/2	cup raisins

Preheat the oven to 350°.

Beat the eggs until fluffy, then beat in the sugar, oil, and honey. Blend in the mango. In a separate bowl, combine the flour, baking soda, cinnamon, and salt. Add the dry ingredients to the egg mixture, combine, and stir in the vanilla, walnuts, and raisins.

Pour the batter into 2 greased 8 1/2 x 4 1/4-inch or 9 x 5-inch loaf pans. Bake 40 to 45 minutes or until the bread springs back to the touch and a tester comes out clean. Let the loaves stand for 20 minutes before removing them from the pans.

Note: 3 to 4 mangoes will yield the 2 cups you need for this recipe. As you cut up the mango, be careful not to include any of the fibrous matter near the pit .

Yield: 2 loaves.

Apple Fritters

Serve this as an hors d'oeuvre for brunch or as the breakfast fruit.

- 1½ cups all-purpose flour
- 2 tablespoons sugar
- 2 tablespoons baking powder
- 1 cup milk
- 1 egg, beaten
- 4 cups apples, peeled, cored, and chopped into 1-inch pieces (4 to 6 medium)
- 1½ cups peanut oil
- ¼ cup sugar
- 1 teaspoon cinnamon

Mix together the flour, sugar, and baking powder and combine with the milk and egg. Mix in the chopped apples.

Heat the oil in a deep-sided skillet to 365°, or until a 1-inch cube of bread browns in 60 seconds.

Drop the batter by tablespoonfuls into the hot oil and cook until golden. Drain the fritters on paper towels. Combine the sugar and cinnamon and sprinkle over the fritters.

Yield: About 40 fritters.

The Gables

LENOX, MASSACHUSETTS

Pulitzer prize-winning novelist Edith Wharton once lived in this multi-gabled 1885 house, and she wrote in its eight-sided library. The inn is in the heart of the Berkshire mountains where the Boston Symphony Orchestra makes its home at Tanglewood.

Morning Zucchini Bread

It is believed that this recipe, which has stayed with the house, was served to Edith Wharton for breakfast.

- 1 cup sugar
- 1/2 cup vegetable oil
- 2 eggs
- 1 teaspoon baking powder
- 2 teaspoons baking soda
- 1 teaspoon salt
- 1 teaspoon vanilla extract
- 1/4 teaspoon cinnamon
- 1/4 teaspoon ground cloves
- 1 cup shredded zucchini (1 medium)
- 2 cups all-purpose flour

Preheat the oven to 400°.

Mix together all the ingredients in order, and bake in a greased 9 x 5-inch loaf pan for 50 minutes or until a tester comes out clean.

Yield: 1 loaf.

Cornucopia

DORSET, VERMONT

Rambling around southwestern Vermont one warm summer's day, I spotted a motor vehicle with the license plate BNB INN. Intrigued, I followed the moving sign all the way to a quaint house and found the Cornucopia Bed & Breakfast. Bill and Linda Ley have a comfortable and inviting inn with some of the most comfortable bedclothes anywhere!

Croissants à l'Orange

Show-stopper is one way to describe this unusual dessert-like dish which you can prepare the night before.

- 6 large croissants, cut into top and bottom halves
- 1 jar (18-ounces) orange marmalade
- 1/3 cup orange juice
- 5 large eggs
- 1 cup heavy cream
- 1 teaspoon almond extract
- 1 teaspoon grated orange rind (optional)
- 3 orange slices, for garnish
- whipped cream, for garnish
- 6 strawberries, for garnish

Grease 6 oven-proof bowls big enough to hold one croissant each (about 6 inches in diameter). Place the bottom half of a croissant in each bowl. Thin the marmalade with the orange juice and spoon 2 to 3 tablespoonfuls over each bottom, according to the sweetness desired. Replace the croissant tops. Beat together the eggs, cream and almond extract, add the orange rind if desired, and pour about 3 tablespoonfuls of the mixture over each croissant. Spoon 1 to 2 tablespoonfuls of the remaining marmalade mixture over the top of each.

Cover the croissants and let soak overnight. Bake in a preheated 350° oven for 20 to 25 minutes or until the mixture is set. Serve the croissants hot, allowing them a few minutes to settle. Garnish each serving with a half slice of orange and a tablespoon of whipped cream topped with a strawberry.

Yield: 6 servings.

The Governor's Inn

LUDLOW, VERMONT

Innkeepers Deedy and Charlie Marble are chefs as well as hospitality experts, and the Governor's Inn has received many culinary awards. You might have seen their inn on the back of the Broccoli Rice au Gratin package, one of Uncle Ben's Country Inn Rice Dishes.™

The Governor's Peach Pudding

"We love the idea of pudding at breakfast," says Deedy. We do, too.

- 2 cups sour cream
- 1/2 cup sugar
- 1 tablespoon all-purpose flour
- 1 teaspoon nutmeg
- 1/4 teaspoon maple extract
- 2 cans (1 pound each) sliced peaches, drained and cut into small chunks
- 1 cup chopped nuts
- 1/2 cup raisins

Preheat the oven to 375°.

In a medium bowl, mix together the first five ingredients. Fold in the peaches and pour the batter into a greased 8-inch square baking pan. Sprinkle with nuts and raisins (or top with an equivalent amount of müesli cereal). Bake for 45 minutes or until golden brown. Let the pudding cool slightly and serve in small bowls.

Yield: 8 servings.

Maple Porridge

When the U.S. Department of Agriculture was looking for recipes using Vermont maple syrup for a worldwide promotion, Charlie's recipe was among those chosen.

- 1 1/2 teaspoons salt
- 3 1/4 cups old-fashioned oatmeal
- 2 cups milk
- 4 large eggs, beaten
- 1 cup pure Vermont maple syrup
- 1/2 cup dark molasses
- 1/2 cup dark brown sugar
- 1 1/3 cups dark raisins
- 1/2 cup chopped walnuts
- 1 teaspoon cinnamon
- 1 teaspoon ground ginger
- 1/2 teaspoon nutmeg
- vanilla ice cream and Vermont maple syrup, as accompaniments

Preheat the oven to 350°.

Bring 1 1/2 quarts water to a boil in a large pot and add the salt and oatmeal. Reduce the heat and cook for 5 minutes, then remove the pot from the heat and cool. Combine the remaining ingredients, except for the ice cream and maple syrup, and mix them into the cooled oatmeal.

Pour the mixture into a greased 9 x 13-inch baking pan. Bake the porridge for 1 hour or until it is set. Serve hot in warmed cereal bowls, topped with a scoop of vanilla ice cream covered with maple syrup.

Yield: 4 to 6 servings.

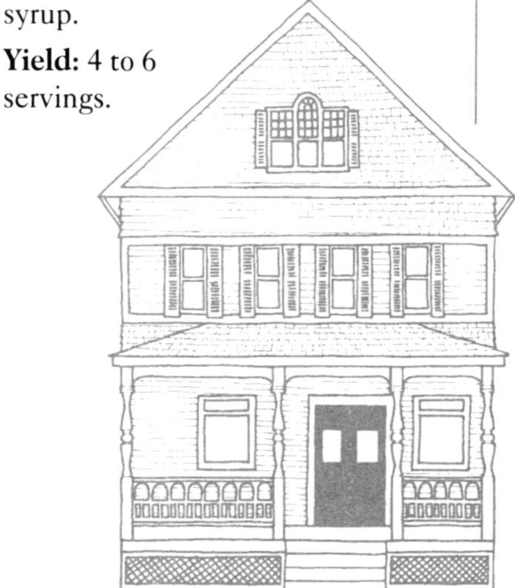

Windham Hill

WEST TOWNSHEND, VERMONT

There's always something cooking at Windham Hill—usually something award-winning, as the inn's plaques can attest. But there are also the events innkeepers Linda and Ken Busteed are continually planning, such as jazz dances and chamber music concerts. Not to mention that Windham Hill has its own cross-country ski learning center. This is a classic country inn; guest service is paramount, with the owners/innkeepers always on hand, and the food has been applauded nationwide.

HAM AND CHEESE OMELET ROLL

This is what you call a genuine egg roll. Your guests will express surprise and delight, especially when you serve it with Windham Hill's Mushroom Timbales.

- 12 eggs
- 1/2 teaspoon salt
- 1/4 teaspoon pepper
- Dijon-style mustard
- 1/2 pound thinly sliced ham
- 1/2 pound thinly sliced Swiss cheese
- 1 cup chopped scallions with tops (about 1 bunch)

Preheat the oven to 350°.

Lightly grease a 10 x 15-inch jelly roll pan, and line it with greased wax paper.

Combine the eggs, salt and pepper, beating well. Pour the mixture into the prepared pan and bake for 10 to 15 minutes, or until the omelet is set.

When the eggs are done, invert them onto a piece of foil and gently peel off the wax paper. Spread a thin layer of mustard on the baked eggs. Layer with thinly sliced ham and Swiss cheese and top with the chopped scallions. Roll up the omelet jelly roll fashion and wrap it tightly in foil. Place the roll on a cookie sheet and return it to the oven for 10 minutes. Remove the foil, slice the omelet roll and serve.

Yield: 6 to 8 servings.

Windham Hill

WEST TOWNSHEND, VERMONT

Mushroom Ragout Timbales

Each August, Windham Hill holds its Mushroom Hunting Weekend, which starts with an informative lecture about mushrooms. On Saturday, guests hike around the inn and further afield, learning to find and identify mushroom varieties ranging from porcinis to chanterelles. The event is led and carefully supervised by fungi experts Harry and Rosalind Lustig. Edible guest finds are cooked up by the innkeepers for breakfast or dinner.

- 1/2 cup unsalted butter
- 1 large onion, minced
- 2 cloves garlic, minced
- 1 1/2 pounds thinly sliced mushrooms
- 4 eggs
- 1 cup milk
- 6 slices French bread, crusts trimmed, cut into cubes (about 1 cup)
- 1/2 teaspoon nutmeg
- 1/2 teaspoon ground red pepper
- 1/2 teaspoon salt
- 1/2 teaspoon freshly ground pepper

Preheat the oven to 350°. Grease eight 6-ounce ramekins.

Melt the butter in a large skillet over medium heat. Add the onions and garlic and sauté until tender. Add the mushrooms and cook for another 3 to 5 minutes. Combine the eggs and milk and beat well. Stir in the bread cubes and blend in the seasonings. Add the mushroom mixture and stir gently. Spoon into the prepared dishes and bake for 30 to 40 minutes or until set.

Yield: 8 servings.

WINDHAM HILL INN

Mid-
Atlantic

The Village Victorian Inn at Rhinebeck

RHINEBECK, NEW YORK

The Village Victorian is a classic 1860 residence in view of the Hudson River. You can spend the day watching the river run or exploring the village of Rhinebeck with its quaint shops and restaurants. Rooms at the inn are very period and most comfortable. Innkeeper Judy Kohler has treated her inn to Oriental rugs, fine linens and fancy laces. Breakfast is always a full one and there are often specials, including the inn's famous cheese blintzes and fresh trout caught by the chef.

Banana Sour Cream Waffles

These waffles have a light texture but wonderfully intense flavor, thanks to the banana. Maple syrup served overtop is a wonderful complement to the fruit.

1	cup all-purpose flour
1/2	teaspoon baking powder
1/4	teaspoon baking soda
1/4	teaspoon salt
1	egg, separated
1	cup sour cream
1/4	cup milk
1/4	cup butter, melted
1	ripe banana, mashed

Sift together the dry ingredients and set aside. Beat the egg yolks until well combined. Whip the egg whites until light peaks form. In a bowl, mix together the egg yolks, sour cream, milk, butter, and banana. Add to the flour mixture, mixing well. Fold in the whipped egg white.

Pour the batter into a greased and heated waffle iron and cook until golden, or according to waffle iron directions.

Yield: 6-8 waffles.

The Queen Victoria

CAPE MAY, NEW JERSEY

Breakfast at "The Queen," so-called by enamored locals, is a fabulous affair. Everyone sits at an antique table that stretches across the dining room, after helping themselves to an assortment of fresh-baked goodies on a breakfast buffet. Innkeepers Joan and Dane Wells are veteran hosts who make you feel as though you are their very first guest. Joan and I are kindred spirits, brought together by our mutual affection for egg cups. One day, Joan brought up boxes of wrapped egg cups she hadn't looked at in years. She showed childish delight in giving me a tour of her collection. Other breakfast guests joined in. What a treat! If you ask, maybe she'll serve you a soft-boiled egg in one of them.

Pineapple and Nut Cheese Spread

I can't think of a better nutritional alternative to butter in the morning than this delightful combination on whole wheat toast, bagels, or muffins. You may substitute neufchâtel for the cream cheese. Joan and Dane also serve this spread with crackers during tea time.

16	ounces cream cheese, very soft
1	can (8 1/2 ounces) crushed pineapple, drained, or 1 cup crushed fresh pineapple
1/3	cup chopped pecans or almonds
1/4	cup diced green bell pepper
2	tablespoons diced green onion

In a large bowl, mix together all ingredients. Cover and chill 3 to 4 hours or overnight. Set out at room temperature before serving.

The mixture can also be formed into a ball and rolled in an additional 1 cup of nuts.

Yield: 1 1/2 cups.

The Cabbage Rose Inn

FLEMINGTON, NEW JERSEY

"Finding recipes that are easy to make and leave our guests in awe is a continuing challenge," confides innkeeper Pam Venosa. And her challenges extend well beyond the kitchen. As part of their restoration of the inn, she and husband Al Scott spent painstaking days just removing foam-backed carpet that had been glued to the oak plank floors. Cabbage roses are scattered about the inn in many forms; they even appear on the elegant wrapping of the boxed chocolates Pam makes and sells.

Applebake with Granola and Vanilla Yogurt

A delicious, healthy, elegant meal all in one dish!

- 8 medium red apples, pared, cored and cut into 1/2-inch chunks
- 1/3 cup water
- 1/3 cup sugar
- 1 teaspoon cinnamon
- 1/2 teaspoon nutmeg
- 1 cup granola
- 2 cups vanilla yogurt

Combine the apples and water in a 2-quart microwave-safe dish. Cover and microwave on high for 12 to 14 minutes or until the apples are tender. Stir 2 or 3 times while cooking. Stir in the remaining ingredients except granola and yogurt, cover and microwave on high for 2 to 4 minutes or until the sugar dissolves. Stir well.

Spoon the applebake into serving dishes, sprinkle with granola and add a dollop of vanilla yogurt.

Yield: 8 to 10 servings.

Italian Plum Coffee Cake

This plum cake is delicious with a cup of Redstone Amaretto Coffee on page 69.

1/2	cup unsalted butter
1	cup sugar
2	eggs
2	cups sifted, unbleached flour
1	teaspoon baking powder
1/8	teaspoon salt
12	Italian or purple plums, halved and pitted
2	tablespoons sugar
1/2	teaspoon cinnamon

Preheat the oven to 350°.

Cream together the butter and sugar. Add the eggs and beat well. Stir in the flour, baking powder and salt, and mix only to combine. Spoon the batter into a greased 9-inch springform pan, and place the plums, skin-side up, on top. Combine the sugar and cinnamon and sprinkle lightly over the batter.

Bake the cake for 1 hour or until the crust is golden and a tester comes out clean. Serve warm.

Yield: 8 wedges.

Apple Bread Pudding

Baking apples in a pudding is a delicious way to use the fruit when it's not at its peak.

- 8 slices white or whole-wheat bread, toasted and cut into fourths
- 4 medium red apples, peeled and cored
- 1/2 cup golden raisins
- 1 1/3 cups milk
- 1/2 cup butter
- 5 eggs, beaten
- 1/2 cup sugar
- 1/2 teaspoon cinnamon
- 1/4 teaspoon nutmeg
- 1/4 teaspoon salt
- 1/4 cup firmly packed dark brown sugar
- 1 quart half and half

Preheat the oven to 350°.

Arrange some of the bread in a single layer in a buttered 11 x 7 x 2-inch baking dish. Slice 1 apple and dice the remaining 3 to equal about 4 cups. Spread the diced apples evenly over the bread, followed by the raisins. Arrange the remaining bread in 2 lengthwise rows down the middle of the pan. Place the apple slices between the rows of bread.

In a small saucepan, over medium heat, heat the milk and butter until the butter melts. In a large bowl, combine the eggs, sugar, spices, and salt, and gradually add the milk mixture, stirring constantly. Pour the mixture over the bread and apples and top with the brown sugar. Bake for 40 minutes or until set. Serve the bread pudding warm, with half and half.

Yield: 8 to 10 servings.

Cabbage Rose Granola

Honey has greater sweetening power than sugar. It gives this granola a woodsy flavor.

- 2 cups oats (old-fashioned or quick)
- 1/2 cup unsalted sunflower seeds
- 1/2 cup flaked coconut
- 1/2 cup wheat germ
- 1 teaspoon cinnamon
- 1/2 cup whole almonds or pecan halves
- 1/4 cup vegetable oil
- 1/4 cup honey
- 1 teaspoon vanilla extract
- 1/2 cup raisins

Preheat the oven to 325°.

In a large bowl, mix together the dry ingredients. In a small saucepan, combine the oil, honey and vanilla, and heat until boiling. Stir the mixture into the dry ingredients, combine well, and spread on an ungreased jelly roll pan.

Place the pan in the middle of the oven rack and bake the granola until golden, about 20 to 30 minutes, stirring away from the edges every 10 minutes. Remove the granola from the oven and mix in the raisins. Cool before storing.

Yield: 8 servings.

The Blushing Rose

HAMMONDSPORT, NEW YORK

The Blushing Rose, as its name implies, is an attractively decorated Bed-and-Breakfast. Innkeepers Ellen and Bucky Laufersweiler run things in a lighthearted manner, and that spirit is transmitted to their guests. Located in the Finger Lakes, the inn is close to nature, wineries and museums. A few of the inn's recipes are printed on stationery cards and offered for sale.

Lemon Yogurt Poppy Seed Waffles

Most poppy seeds are brought here from Holland for use in dishes such as these light and tasty waffles.

- 2 eggs, lightly beaten
- 2 cups baking mix, such as Bisquick™
- 2 cartons (8 ounces each) lemon yogurt
- 1/2 cup corn or canola oil
- 2 teaspoons poppy seed
- pancake syrup as an accompaniment
- additional lemon yogurt and grated lemon peel, for garnish

Coat a waffle iron with non-stick spray.

In a large bowl, combine the first five ingredients, stirring just until combined. Batter will be lumpy. Ladle 1/4 cup of batter onto the griddle, or more or less according to the iron's size. Bake the waffles 4 to 5 minutes or until golden, or until the iron indicates doneness. Serve hot with syrup, garnished with lemon yogurt and lemon peel.

Yield: 16 waffles.

Orange Oatmeal Pie

An unusual way to eat traditional oatmeal. For a low-fat version, omit the pie shell.

- 3/4 cup skim milk
- 3 eggs, beaten
- 1/2 cup orange juice
- 1/4 cup sugar (or 2 tablespoons honey)
- 1/2 cup quick oats
- 2 tablespoons margarine, melted and cooled
- 1 9-inch precooked pie shell (optional)
- yogurt of any flavor as an accompaniment

Preheat the oven to 350°.

Mix together all the ingredients except the pie shell and yogurt. Pour the batter into the pie shell (or cook without a shell in a pie pan or quiche dish that has been coated with non-stick spray).

Bake the pie for 35 to 40 minutes or until it is set. Serve in wedges, topped with the yogurt.

Yield: 8 wedges.

BLUSHING ROSE FEATHERBED EGGS

This recipe is nice because you make it ahead, refrigerate overnight, and bake in the morning.

6	slices bread, buttered
	salt and pepper
1 1/2	cups grated Cheddar cheese
1 1/2	cups milk
6	eggs

Arrange the bread in a 9 x 13-inch baking dish that has been coated with non-stick spray. Salt and pepper the bread lightly and sprinkle the cheese on top. Combine the milk and eggs and pour over.

Cover the dish and refrigerate overnight. Place in a cold oven, set temperature at 350° and bake for 1 hour, or until puffed and golden. Serve immediately.

Yield: 6 servings.

Goose Chase

GARDNERS, PENNSYLVANIA

Breakfast on this gentleman's farm is gourmet. Innkeepers Marsha and Rich Lucidi hold cooking classes on special weekends for guests who want to pick up a spatula as well as a fork. Folk art, American country antiques, wide-board floors and deep-silled windows, all combined in an 18th-century stone house, are the signature of this B&B and a doorway to another time and place. The Lucidis often dress in period garb (see back cover).

Fruit and Cheese Pizza

Served instead of muffins, this sweet rendition of the circular dough-topped savory is a formidable treat.

- 1 package (20 ounces) sugar cookie dough
- 8 ounces cream cheese
- 1/3 cup sugar
- 1/2 teaspoon vanilla extract
- 4 cups of any combination of fresh fruit, cut up
- 1/2 cup apricot preserves
- 3 tablespoons brandy

Preheat the oven to 375°.

Slice the cookie dough into 1/4-inch thick rounds and arrange them on a lightly oiled 12-inch pizza pan, overlapping slightly, until the pan is covered completely. Press the dough together to seal. Bake the dough round for 10 minutes or until it is lightly browned. Cool completely.

Combine the cream cheese, sugar, and vanilla and spread evenly over the cookie crust. (The pizza may be made a day ahead to this point and refrigerated, covered.)

Arrange the fruit in a circular pattern over the filling. In a small saucepan, melt the apricot preserves with the brandy, and brush the preserves over the fruit. Chill for 1 hour. Cut the pizza into wedges to serve.

Yield: 12 servings.

Open-Faced Breakfast Tortillas

The family will be saying "olé" instead of "good morning!"

- 6 small flour tortillas
- 3 tablespoons butter
- 12 large eggs
- 3/4 teaspoon salt
- 1/2 teaspoon black pepper
- 1 can or jar (2 ounces) chopped green chilies, drained
- 3/4 cup sliced green onions
- 1 1/2 cups shredded cheddar cheese
- 1 avocado, sliced
- 3/4 cup salsa
- 1/2 cup sour cream

Preheat the oven to 350°.

Place the tortillas on an ungreased baking sheet and warm them in the oven for about 5 minutes. Melt the butter in a large skillet. In a large bowl, beat the eggs, adding the salt, pepper, and chilies. Pour the egg mixture into the skillet and scramble the eggs until they are set but still soft. Stir in the onions and spoon the eggs onto the warmed tortillas. Sprinkle the eggs with cheese and top each tortilla with 2 avocado slices, 2 tablespoons salsa and a dollop of sour cream.

Yield: 6 servings.

APPLE DUMPLINGS WITH SPICY RUM SAUCE

Goose Chase, located on Blueberry Road, is surrounded by apple orchards. Naturally, fruit often graces the breakfast table. These dumplings are easy to do and look impressive.

Sauce

- 1 cup apple juice
- 1/4 cup dark rum
- 1/4 cup butter
- 1/4 teaspoon cinnamon
- 1/4 teaspoon nutmeg

Dumplings

- 2 cups all-purpose flour
- 2 teaspoons baking powder
- 1/2 teaspoon salt
- 2/3 cup solid vegetable shortening
- 1/2 cup ice cold milk
- 4 large Rome apples, cored and peeled
- 1/4 cup sugar
- 1/4 cup heavy cream

To make the sauce, combine the juice, rum, butter, cinnamon and nutmeg in a small saucepan over medium heat. Cook until the butter melts, but do not boil. Keep stirring for 5 minutes over low heat to let the alcohol burn off, then remove from heat.

Preheat the oven to 375°.

Sift together the flour, baking powder and salt. Cut in the shortening until mixture resembles coarse meal. Pour in the milk and mix only long enough to create a ragged dough.

Gather the dough into a ball on a well-floured surface. Sprinkling flour over the top of the dough as needed, roll the dough into a 16-inch square. Cut the dough into 4 even squares. Place an apple in the center of each and sprinkle with 1 tablespoon of sugar. Wrap the dough around each apple, pinching and sealing on all sides.

Place the dumplings in an 8-inch square baking dish and pour the rum sauce over them. Bake the dumplings for 25 minutes, basting 4 or 5 times with sauce. Stir the cream into the sauce in the pan and bake 15 minutes more, or until the dumplings are golden brown. Remove the dumplings from the oven, place in individual serving bowls and drizzle with the sauce.

Yield: 4 dumplings.

Strawberry Bread with Strawberry Cream Cheese

The creamy spread doubles the berry rich taste of this luscious fruity bread. Your guests will glow on their way out the door.

3	cups all-purpose flour
1	teaspoon baking soda
1/2	teaspoon salt
1	teaspoon cinnamon
2	cups sugar
2	packages (10 ounces each) frozen strawberries, thawed, drained, juice reserved
3	large eggs, beaten
1	cup vegetable oil
1	cup chopped pecans

Strawberry Cream Cheese

8	ounces cream cheese, softened
1/2	cup reserved strawberry juice

Preheat the oven to 350°.

Mix together the flour, baking soda, salt, cinnamon, and sugar. Make a deep well in the center of the mixture and pour in the strawberries, eggs, oil and pecans. Mix by hand until all ingredients are thoroughly combined, and pour the mixture into 2 greased 9 x 5-inch loaf pans. Bake 45 to 50 minutes or until a tester comes out clean. Remove the loaves from the pans and cool on wire racks.

For the strawberry cream cheese, combine the cream cheese with the reserved strawberry juice. Serve on cooled, sliced bread.

Yield: 2 loaves.

Swiss Woods

LITITZ, PENNSYLVANIA

It's not the Swiss Alps, but it's the next best thing. Swiss Woods is perched on a hillside overlooking a rural lake and forest. Everything is Old World, from the bark-cut coffee tables to the Swiss bread pastries. The inn, owned by Debra and Werner Mosimann, is modeled after chalets in Switzerland, where the couple lived for five years. Special dinners, such as fondues, are on the menu in winter by special reservation.

BIRCHERMÜESLI

Dr. Max Bircher of Switzerland created this breakfast dish in the early 1900s. He was a firm believer in the healing advantages of raw vegetables and fruits. The owners of Swiss Woods say it's still that country's most popular breakfast treat.

1	cup oats, quick and old-fashioned mixed
1/2	cup plain yogurt
	juice of 1 lemon
2/3	cup milk
1/4	cup sugar
1	apple, cored and coarsely grated
1	peach, pitted, sliced and cubed
1/2	cup white or red seedless grapes, halved
1	can (11 ounces) mandarin oranges, drained
1	pear, cored and chopped
1	cup fresh strawberries, cleaned, hulled, and thinly sliced
1/2	cup chopped hazelnuts or almonds
1/4	cup raisins
1/2	cup freshly whipped cream

Combine the oats, yogurt, lemon juice, milk, and sugar. Add the fruits and nuts. Just before serving, fold in the whipped cream.

Yield: 12 servings.

Blueberry Poppy Seed Brunch Cake with Lemon Curd

Lemon curd is used enthusiastically by the British as a sweet condiment. In addition to serving it with the cake, you can spread it on your morning toast.

- 2/3 cup sugar
- 1/2 cup butter
- 1 egg
- 2 teaspoons grated lemon peel
- 1 1/2 cups all-purpose flour
- 2 tablespoons poppy seed
- 1/2 teaspoon baking soda
- 1/2 cup sour cream
- 2 cups fresh blueberries
- 1 tablespoon all-purpose flour
- 1/4 teaspoon nutmeg
- Lemon Curd (recipe at right)

Preheat the oven to 350°.

Beat together the sugar and butter in a large bowl until fluffy. Add the egg and lemon peel and beat for 2 minutes at medium speed. In a separate bowl, mix together the 1 1/2 cups flour, poppy seeds, and baking soda, and set aside. Add the dry ingredients and the sour cream alternately to the butter mixture and combine.

In another bowl, mix together the blueberries, the tablespoon of flour and the nutmeg. Fold this mixture into the batter. Spread the batter in an ungreased 9-inch square pan. Bake for 35 to 45 minutes or until a tester comes out clean. Serve the cake with Lemon Curd on the side.

Yield: 8 to 10 servings.

Lemon Curd

- 5 lemons
- 1 cup sugar
- 1 cup butter, cut into pieces
- 5 eggs

Grate the rind from the lemons and set it aside. Juice the lemons to yield about 2/3 cup liquid. Pour the juice into a blender, add the sugar, butter and eggs and whirl until well mixed. Pour the mixture into the top of a 2-quart double boiler and stir in the grated rind. Cook the mixture over hot (not boiling) water, stirring constantly until all the butter is melted and the mixture becomes very thick and creamy, about 15 minutes. Cool the lemon curd completely and refrigerate for 6 hours or overnight before serving.

Yield: Approximately 2 cups.

The Whitehall Inn

NEW HOPE, PENNSYLVANIA

Breakfast at this 1794 inn is four courses accompanied by more flickering candles than I've ever seen glowing at one time, except at church. Breakfast at the Whitehall is so divine that it would probably even delight residents of heaven. Innkeepers Mike and Suella Wass offer a mouthwatering mosaic of recipes by Suella, served against a background of crisp white linen, European china, shimmering crystal and intricately patterned heirloom sterling. You'll never eat the same thing twice here. Suella keeps copious records on who was served what and she refers to them often as guests return again and again.

Apple Paprika Soup

"The paprika used in the recipe is the sweet kind," says Mike. "Not the kind you normally associate with deviled eggs."

- 4 baking apples, peeled, cored and chopped
- 2 1/2 cups water
- 1/2 cup sugar
- 2 tablespoons fresh lemon juice
- 2 teaspoons sweet paprika
- 1 cinnamon stick (2 inches)
- 2 whole cloves
- 1/4 teaspoon freshly grated nutmeg
- thin, peeled apple slices for garnish

Combine all ingredients except sliced apples in a large saucepan. Simmer the mixture, covered, until the apples are very tender, about 20 minutes. Remove the cinnamon stick and cloves and purée the mixture in a blender until smooth. Serve the soup warm with the sliced apples on the side.

Yield: 4 to 6 servings.

Cinnamon Rolls

Cinnamon comes from the bark of trees on Ceylon, the Malabar Coast, and Saigon. We are thankful it reaches these shores to make possible this rendition of cinnamon rolls by The Whitehall.

- 2 packages (1/4 ounce each) fast-acting yeast
- 1/2 cup lukewarm water
- 1 cup buttermilk, room temperature
- 3 tablespoons sugar
- 2 teaspoons salt
- 4 cups all-purpose flour
- 4 egg yolks
- 1 cup very soft butter
- 2 tablespoons butter, melted
- 1/3 cup sugar
- 1 tablespoon cinnamon

Icing

- 1/2 cup butter
- 1/4 cup half and half
- 1 teaspoon vanilla extract
- 2 1/2 cups confectioners' sugar

Dissolve the yeast in the lukewarm water. Combine the yeast mixture with the buttermilk, sugar, salt, flour, and egg yolks in a mixer with a dough hook (or mix by hand in a bowl, using a wooden spoon). Beat until a smooth dough has formed, then slowly add the softened butter. Continue to beat the mixture on high for 8 to 10 minutes until it is smooth and pulls away from the bowl. Cover the dough and refrigerate for 6 hours.

Roll out the dough on a floured surface to a 20 x 10-inch rectangle. Brush it with the melted butter and sprinkle with the sugar and cinnamon mixed together. Evenly roll the dough lengthwise, jelly roll style, finishing with the seam side down. Slice the roll into 1 1/2-inch thick rounds and place them 1 1/2 inches apart on a baking sheet coated with non-stick spray. Cover the rolls and let them rise until doubled. Bake in a preheated 350° oven for 15 to 20 minutes or until golden. Let cool.

Combine all the icing ingredients in a mixer bowl. Beat for 5 minutes or until smooth. Spread the icing over the rolls while they are still warm.

Yield: 12 rolls.

Butter Coffee Cake

Cream cheese enriches the topping of this very moist, pudding-like cake. If you like, add a few drops of yellow food coloring to the batter to perk up this or any coffee or pound cake.

- 2 cups all-purpose flour
- 1 1/2 cups sugar
- 1 tablespoon baking powder
- 1 teaspoon salt
- 3 tablespoons shortening
- 5 eggs
- 1/2 cup butter, melted
- 8 ounces cream cheese
- 1 pound confectioners sugar
- 1 1/2 tablespoons vanilla extract

Preheat the oven to 350°.

Combine the flour, sugar, baking powder, and salt and cut in the shortening with a pastry blender or in a food processor until the mixture resembles coarse meal. Mix in 3 of the eggs and the butter and combine well. Spread this batter over the bottom of a greased 9 x 13-inch baking pan.

Combine the cream cheese, the 2 remaining eggs, the sugar (reserving two tablespoons) and the vanilla, and pour this mixture over the batter in the baking pan. Bake the cake for 15 minutes, remove from the oven and sprinkle the reserved sugar over the top. Return the cake to the oven and bake for 35 minutes more. When done, the cake will still be moist in the center. Cool slightly before serving.

Yield: 10 to 12 servings.

Apple Butter French Toast

When leaves start falling, you'll want to whip up this seasonal French toast.

- 8 slices French bread, 3/4-inch thick
- 6 eggs, beaten
- 3/4 cup apple cider
- 1/3 cup milk
- 1/4 teaspoon vanilla extract
- 4 ounces cream cheese, softened
- 2 tablespoons apple butter
- 1/4 cup or more unseasoned dry bread crumbs
- confectioners' sugar or maple syrup

Make a pocket in each bread slice by slicing almost completely through. Mix together the eggs, cider, milk, and vanilla. In another bowl, mix the cream cheese and apple butter. Spread some of the apple butter mixture inside each bread pocket. Place the stuffed pieces into a pan or casserole dish just big enough to hold them and pour the apple cider mixture over them. Turn to coat each side. Cover and refrigerate for several hours or overnight.

Preheat the oven to 350°.

Sprinkle a thin layer of bread crumbs over the stuffed bread slices and place them crumb-side down on a greased 9 x 13-inch baking pan. Bake the slices 10 to 15 minutes or until they are lightly browned, rotating the pan so the bread will brown evenly. Turn the slices over and continue baking for 10 minutes more. Arrange the toast on a plate and sprinkle with confectioners sugar or maple syrup.

Yield: 4 servings.

The Shadows

ORANGE, VIRGINIA

Pat Loffredo retired from the New York City Police Department in search of a quieter life. But he's still policing—in the kitchen that is—as he serves up breakfast with his wife, Barbara. The inn is friendly and decorated with antiques. (Ask Barbara about her collection of glove molds.) The Rose Room, with its clawfoot tub, is a personal favorite of mine. After a day of sightseeing, which might include the restored home of James and Dolly Madison, the special pampering here is most welcome.

Poached Pears with Grand Marnier Cream

The inn follows this pear dish with stuffed French toast.

- 8 fresh pears
- 1/2 gallon orange or pineapple juice, or a combination
- 1/2 cup heavy cream, whipped
- 1 cup vanilla ice cream, slightly softened
- 2 tablespoons Grand Marnier
- 1/4 cup grated orange rind, or to taste
- fresh mint for garnish

Cut a thin slice from the bottom of each pear so it will stand upright. Core the pears from the bottom, leaving the stems intact, and peel them. Place the pears in a 4-quart pot and add the juice. Bring to a boil and cook until the pears are springy when squeezed (about 5 to 7 minutes for ripe pears).

Remove the pears and stand each in a bowl. Mix together the whipped cream (or a commercially prepared cream), ice cream, and the liqueur until the mixture is soft. Spoon some of the cream mixture over each pear, sprinkle grated orange rind over the tops and garnish with fresh mint.

Yield: 8 servings.

Newport House

WILLIAMSBURG, VIRGINIA

Breakfast is a historically spirited one at Newport House. Innkeepers John and Cathy Millar serve 18th-century fare at their 1756 reproduction home. John, a historian, presides at the table with tales of America's early swashbuckling days. Cathy sews Colonial garb that guests may rent for sightseeing, wearing at dinner, or for chasséing on Tuesdays when she teaches Colonial country dancing in the inn's ballroom. Newport House is a five-minute stroll from Williamsburg's restored village.

Rum Cornmeal Johnnycakes

In Colonial America, rum was added to cornmeal as a preservative. In these egg-free pancakes, it's added for flavor. (When you visit, ask John to explain how rum in johnnycakes was a major cause of the American Revolution.) You may substitute other cornmeal in these cakes, but for authentic taste and best results, order johnnycake cornmeal from:

Carpenter's Grist Mill
35 Narragansett Avenue
Wakefield, RI 02879

- 1 cup johnnycake cornmeal
- 1 tablespoon sugar
- 1/4 teaspoon salt
- 1 cup boiling water
- 2 tablespoons milk
- 1 tablespoon light rum, plus more for thinning
- butter and molasses or maple syrup for serving

Heat a greased griddle to 350°, or until hot but not smoking.

Combine the cornmeal, sugar, and salt in a bowl and pour in the boiling water. Stir in the milk, then the rum, adding enough additional milk or rum to create the consistency of very thin mashed potatoes—as much as 10 tablespoons if needed.

Drop batter onto the griddle by tablespoonfuls for 2-inch cakes. Cook the cakes for one minute on each side or until they are cooked inside and a brown crunchy crust forms. Serve hot with butter and molasses or maple syrup.

Yield: 8 to 10 two-inch cakes.

South

Florida House Inn

AMELIA ISLAND, FLORIDA

Bob and Karen Warner dropped out of corporate life to restore this classic 1857 Victorian inn by the sea. A hearty farmhouse breakfast is served, giving guests energy for browsing beaches, hunting shells, sighting dolphins, shopping for antiques, and then watching shrimp trawlers return with the day's catch as the sun sets.

Apple Pie Pancakes

The Warners serve each of these jumbo pancakes in a larger quiche dish lined with a decorative cloth napkin for warmth and good looks.

- 2 9-inch pie crusts, pre-baked
- 1 can (20 ounces) apple slices (not apple filling), drained
- 2 cups grated sharp cheddar cheese
- 1/4 cup sugar
- 2 teaspoons cinnamon
- 1/2 cup all-purpose flour
- 2 cups milk
- 4 eggs
- maple syrup as an accompaniment

Preheat the oven to 350°.

Divide the apple slices between the pie crusts. Sprinkle each pie evenly with half the cheese, sugar and cinnamon. In a medium bowl, mix the milk gradually into the flour and then whisk in the eggs. Gently pour half of the mixture into each pie.

Bake the pies for 50 minutes or until the filling is set and golden brown. Pie pancakes will be puffy but will deflate once they are out of the oven. Slice the pies and serve with maple syrup.

Yield: 12 to 16 servings.

Sausage and Hash Brown Mini-Frittatas

These make great breakfast hors d'oeuvres and they freeze well. You can also make them in 1¾-inch muffin tins for bite-size pieces, reducing the cooking time to 10 minutes or until they are golden brown.

- 1 pound bulk sausage
- 1 large onion, chopped
- 2 cups frozen hash browns, thawed
- 1 cup grated cheddar cheese
- 3 tablespoons all-purpose flour
- 8 eggs, beaten
- 1 cup ranch-style salad dressing
- ½ cup milk
- salsa as an accompaniment

Preheat the oven to 325°.

In a large skillet over medium heat, sauté the sausage and onion, breaking up the sausage and cooking until the meat is no longer pink. Drain the sausage and let it cool. Transfer the mixture to a large mixing bowl, add the potatoes and cheese and toss to mix. (The recipe can be made one day ahead to this point and refrigerated.) Stir the flour into the mixture. Add the eggs, dressing and milk and stir well. Spoon the mixture into greased muffin tins (2¾-inch), filling each cup halfway. Bake 15 to 20 minutes or until the frittatas are set and golden brown. Serve with warm salsa.

Yield: 24 to 30 mini-frittatas.

Ham and Tarragon Eggs in Puff Pastry

Guests will delight in opening these packages, which ooze with surprises.

6	frozen puff pastry shells, baked according to package directions and kept warm
5	large eggs
3	tablespoons ranch-style salad dressing
1	teaspoon dried tarragon
1/4	cup chopped ham
1/4	cup chopped green onion

Whisk together the eggs, dressing, and tarragon. Fold in the ham and green onion. In a large, non-stick, greased skillet, scramble the egg mixture over low heat. Do not overcook.

Make a pocket in each pastry shell, divide the egg mixture among them and serve. The pastries may be wrapped with foil and kept in a warm oven for a short time, but don't wait too long or they will dry out.

Yield: 6 servings.

Creamy Hash Browns with Chicken, Mushrooms and Cheese

Bob and Karen adapted Bob's mother's recipe for hash browns to come up with this, Florida House's most-requested dish. Prepare it the night before.

- 2 pounds frozen hash browns, thawed
- 1 can condensed cream of mushroom soup
- 1 can condensed cream of chicken soup
- 2 cups grated sharp Cheddar cheese
- 1/2 cup ranch salad dressing
- 1 can (2.8 ounces) fried onion rings

Mix together all ingredients except the onion rings. Cover the mixture and refrigerate overnight.

Next morning, remove the dish from the refrigerator and preheat the oven to 350°.

Pour the potato mixture into a 13 x 9-inch baking dish coated with non-stick spray and bake for 55 minutes or until bubbly. Do not allow the edges to burn. Spread the onion rings over the top of the dish and return to the oven for 5 minutes.

Yield: 12 to 18 servings.

The Gastonian

SAVANNAH, GEORGIA

The gracious South unfolds in regal splendor at this special 1868 home, converted to an inn by Hugh and Roberta Lineberger. Georgian and Regency period antiques abound amid lush wallpapers, draperies, and dramatic art work. Breakfast is southern style and taken ceremoniously in the parlor.

Plantation Eggs and Beef Casserole

This delicious casserole can be frozen.

16	eggs
1	cup evaporated milk
1	tablespoon hot pepper sauce
1/2	teaspoon salt
1/2	cup butter, melted
8	slices bacon
1/2	cup butter
1/2	cup all-purpose flour
1/4	teaspoon ground pepper
1	quart milk
1 1/2	cups mushrooms, trimmed and sliced (about 4 ounces)
1	jar (4 ounces) dried beef, diced
1	jar (2 ounces) pimentos

Preheat the oven to 275°.

Blend the eggs with the evaporated milk, hot pepper sauce and salt. In a large skillet, scramble the eggs in the melted butter until they are soft. Don't overcook. Transfer the eggs to a bowl and set aside.

Cook the bacon in a microwave oven for about 8 minutes or until crisp. Drain the bacon on paper towels and crumble it. Melt all but one tablespoon of the remaining butter in the skillet. Stir in the flour and pepper, and add the milk gradually. Cook, stirring, until smooth. In another skillet, sauté the mushrooms in the remaining tablespoon of butter for 2 to 3 minutes. Add the bacon, mushrooms, beef, and pimentos to the flour and milk mixture and stir well.

Layer the bottom of a greased 9 x 13-inch baking pan with one-third of the beef mixture, then half the scrambled eggs. Repeat, ending with a layer of the beef/sauce mixture on top. Bake 1 hour and 15 minutes.

Yield: 8 servings.

The Lodge on Lake Lure

LAKE LURE, NORTH CAROLINA

Breakfast here is a cotillion of sights, sounds, and scents, served within arm's reach of nature in a glass-enclosed sun porch. The piped-in strains of a hammered dulcimer provide the background to a harmonious homemade meal. Country elegant mixes with mountain casual as innkeepers in jeans preside over crystal goblets at the breakfast table. The area is chockablock with activities to work off the bountiful breakfast.

Buckwheat, Banana and Coconut Pancakes with Mango Sauce

Mangoes are becoming more available, so this recipe makes a nice addition to your pancake repertoire.

2	very ripe bananas
1 1/2	teaspoons fresh lemon juice
1	cup milk (add more for thinner pancakes)
2	egg yolks
3	tablespoons butter, melted
1 1/4	cups buckwheat flour
2	tablespoons sugar
2	teaspoons baking powder
1/4	teaspoon salt
2/3	cup shredded coconut, toasted, for garnish
	Mango Sauce (recipe at right)

Place the bananas and lemon juice in a blender. Add the milk, egg yolks, and butter and blend. In a separate bowl, sift together the flour, sugar, baking powder, and salt. Add the banana mixture to the bowl and combine. Drop batter onto a heated, greased griddle using a 1/4 cup measure to form pancakes. Serve the pancakes with warm Mango Sauce, garnished with coconut.

Yield: 12 4-inch pancakes.

Mango Sauce

1	large ripe mango
1/3	cup sugar
2	tablespoons lemon juice

Peel the mango and cut the flesh into pieces from the fibrous pit, being careful not to include any fibers with the fruit. Process the ingredients in a blender until smooth and simmer in a saucepan over low heat until syrupy.

The Lodge on Lake Lure

LAKE LURE, NORTH CAROLINA

Apple and Sausage Stuffed Croissants

The sweetness and texture of the croissants provide a pleasant variation on this traditional mixture of fruit and meat.

6	tablespoons butter
6	red baking apples, cored, peeled and sliced thin
1	tablespoon curry powder
12	ounces bulk sausage
6	croissants, warmed

In a large skillet, melt the butter and sauté the apples with the curry powder. Remove the mixture from the pan. Cook the sausage in the same skillet until it is lightly browned. Remove the sausage from the pan, drain and combine with the apple mixture. Slice the croissants open and stuff them with the apple/sausage mixture.

Yield: 6 servings.

Cardamom French Toast with Red Currant Syrup

The combination of cardamom and currants results in an interesting marriage of flavors. This is a make-ahead dish.

- 1 1/2 cups milk
- 2 eggs
- 3 tablespoons sugar
- 2 teaspoons grated orange peel
- 1/2 teaspoon vanilla extract
- 1/2 teaspoon salt
- 1/2 teaspoon cardamom
- 12 slices French bread, cut into 3/4-inch pieces
- 1/3 cup butter
- Red Currant Syrup (recipe at right)

Mix together all the ingredients except for the bread and butter. Place the bread in a baking dish, pour the mixture over it, and let it soak overnight. Melt the butter in a large skillet over low heat. Drain the bread and cook slowly in the butter, about 5 minutes on each side. Serve the French toast with Red Currant Jelly Syrup.

Yield: 4 servings of 3 toasts each.

Red Currant Syrup

- 1 cup red currant jelly
- 1/2 cup orange juice
- 3/4 teaspoon cardamom
- 3 tablespoons butter

In a saucepan, heat the jelly with the orange juice and cardamom, stirring occasionally until the jelly is melted. Bring the mixture to a boil and cook until syrupy (about 3 minutes). Remove the syrup from the heat and whip in the butter.

Yield: Approximately 1 1/2 cups.

Mast Farm Inn

VALLE CRUCIS, NORTH CAROLINA

Guest rooms on this 18-acre farm are in a former blacksmith shop, loom house, and woodworker shop. In addition, there is also a spring house, apple house, smoke house, wash house, granary, and barn. A visit to Francis and Sibly Pressly's country inn sends one's imagination reeling. This could be a busy self-sustaining farm circa 1885 representing a German immigrant's dream to build a new life in a new land. Valle Crucis or "vale of the cross," is so called for the three streams that meet here to form a cross.

THREE GRAIN PANCAKES

To reduce cholesterol, use 4 egg whites or an egg substitute instead of whole eggs. Unsweetened applesauce will reduce calories.

- 3 cups buttermilk
- 2 eggs
- 2/3 cup corn oil
- 1/2 cup yellow corn meal
- 1/2 cup unbleached flour
- 1 cup whole-wheat flour
- 1 cup old-fashioned rolled oats
- 2 tablespoons baking powder
- 1/2 teaspoon baking soda
- 1/2 teaspoon salt
- 2 teaspoons sugar (optional)
- maple or fruit syrup or applesauce as accompaniments

Beat together the buttermilk, eggs, and oil in a large bowl. In a separate bowl, mix the dry ingredients well. Add the dry ingredients to the liquid mixture, stirring just enough to blend.

Spray a hot griddle with non-stick spray and drop the pancake batter by tablespoonfuls onto the griddle. Turn only once, when the tops of the pancakes are covered with bubbles. Remove the pancakes to a warm plate when they are browned on the bottom. Serve immediately with maple or fruit syrup and/or applesauce.

Yield: 4 to 6 servings.

McKay House

JEFFERSON, TEXAS

This restored 1851 Greek Revival house is now the inn of Tom and Peggy Taylor. Breakfast is served in period dress and guests may be serenaded with the inn's old pump organ. Jefferson is a riverside town harkening back to frontier days.

McKay House Orange Pecan Toast

Texas is a producer of pecans and oranges, so guests of the inn get a heaping helping of the Lone Star State's best.

- 4 eggs
- 2/3 cup orange juice
- 1/3 cup milk
- 1/4 cup orange liqueur
- 1/4 cup sugar
- 1 tablespoon grated orange rind
- 1/2 teaspoon vanilla extract
- 1/4 teaspoon ground nutmeg
- 1 loaf (8 ounces) Italian or French bread, cut into 1-inch thick slices
- 1/3 cup butter, melted
- 1/2 cup pecans, chopped
- maple syrup, butter and cut up fresh fruit, for serving

Whisk together the eggs, orange juice, milk, liqueur, sugar, grated rind, vanilla and nutmeg. Place the bread in a large casserole or baking pan in a single layer with bread fitting snugly together. Pour the milk mixture over the bread, cover and refrigerate overnight, turning once.

The next morning, preheat the oven to 400°. Pour the melted butter onto a jelly roll pan, spreading it evenly. Arrange the soaked bread slices in a single layer on the pan and sprinkle them with the pecans. Bake the slices for 20 to 25 minutes or until golden. Remove the toasts from the pan to a plate and serve immediately with maple syrup, butter and fresh fruit.

Yield: 4 servings.

Midwest

Maple Leaf Cottage Inn

ELSAH, ILLINOIS

If you've ever dreamed of spending time in a quaint country cottage, Maple Leaf offers several intriguing possibilities, including the Wash House. Originally a summer kitchen in the 1800s, this cottage boasts an antique washing machine, scrubbing board and clothesline that will have you humming the old lyric, "This is the way we wash our clothes, so early in the morning." But as you slip into the white antique iron bed, it's white clouds you'll dream about, not puffs of laundry soap.

CRANAPPLE FRAPPÉ

Serve this refreshing morning beverage in a frosted stem glass.

2	cups cranapple juice
2	ripe bananas
1	cup fresh-squeezed orange juice
3/4	cup crushed ice
1/4	cup whipping cream
1	tablespoon lemon juice
	sugar to taste
3	drops red food coloring

Combine all ingredients in a blender, process for 1 minute and serve.

Yield: Six 6 ounce servings.

Sweet Basil Hill Farm

GURNEE, ILLINOIS

Llamas and sheep roam freely at Bob and Teri Jones' Cape Cod style house and seven-and-a-half acre farm. Guests are invited to pet the animals and run footloose among the farm's fruit groves and vegetable gardens. Bob, an actor and commercial writer, often takes guests on a tour of the farm. Bedrooms in the 1950s house are furnished with antiques and ornamented with Teri's coordinated stenciling.

Basil Buttermilk Scones

There are always plenty of herbs around this inn and Teri makes use of two of them in this recipe. She suggests using an ice cream scoop to drop the scone batter onto the baking sheet.

2	cups unbleached flour
1	cup whole-wheat pastry flour
1/2	teaspoon salt
2 1/2	teaspoons baking powder
1/2	cup butter at room temperature
1	egg
1 1/4	cups buttermilk
2	tablespoons fresh or 1 tablespoon dried basil
2	tablespoons fresh or 1 tablespoon dried parsley
1	egg, beaten

Preheat the oven to 400°.

In a large bowl, mix together the dry ingredients. Cut in the butter with a pastry knife or your fingers until the mixture resembles coarse bread crumbs. In a separate bowl, beat together the egg, buttermilk and herbs, and stir into the flour mixture by hand until it is evenly moistened. Drop scoopfuls of batter 2 inches apart onto a baking sheet coated with non-stick spray. Mix the egg with a tablespoon of water to make an egg wash and brush it over each scone to glaze. Bake the scones for 20 to 25 minutes or until they are golden.

Yield: 12 scones.

The Redstone Inn

DUBUQUE, IOWA

In 1894, industrialist A.A. Cooper built this castle-like Victorian home as a wedding present for his daughter. Today, the inn combines modern-day comforts with Old World antiques. The inn's exterior is sandstone with a red brick gabled roof. Inside, gold-leaf trimmed ceilings and cherry-stained oak woodwork are reminders of Cooper's love for his daughter.

Redstone Amaretto Coffee

The inn serves this creamy, nutty flavored coffee as an encore to a center-stage breakfast.

- 3/4 ounce Irish cream liqueur
- 1/2 ounce amaretto
- 1/2 ounce hazelnut liqueur
- brewed coffee
- whipped cream, for garnish
- red cherry, for garnish

Combine liqueurs in a 6-ounce coffee mug. Pour in hot coffee to fill. Top with whipped cream and a cherry.

Yield: 1 serving.

Victorian Villa

UNION CITY, MICHIGAN

A former professor of the University of Wyoming, Ron Gibson restored his inn with 19th-century wallpaper patterns and rococo and Renaissance furnishings. I love sitting in one of the front parlors, furnished with marble-topped tables and velvety cushioned chairs. The inn hosts several Sherlock Holmes weekends and lots of unusual events all year long, plus afternoon tea every day.

Citrus Mimosa

Almost everybody asks for this recipe, says Ron. To say that this beverage is an eye-opener is an understatement!

- 1 cup prepared strawberry daiquiri mix
- 1 can (6 ounces) frozen orange juice concentrate, thawed
- 3/4 cup water
- 1/3 cup fresh grapefruit juice
- 3 ounces frozen lemonade concentrate, thawed
- 3 ounces frozen limeade concentrate, thawed
- chilled champagne or carbonated water

In a pitcher, combine the daiquiri mix, orange juice concentrate, water, grapefruit juice and lemonade and limeade concentrates. Stir the mixture until well combined. Chill. To serve, fill each glass halfway with the juice mixture and follow with champagne, filling to the top.

Yield: Eight 6-ounce servings.

The Inn at Union Pier

UNION PIER, MICHIGAN

From the moment you first set eyes on this inn via its brochure, you want to visit. A watercolor illustration of a French door literally opens the brochure as you "walk" into the inn. Let this description of The Cottage of the Four Seasons stir your fantasies: "From the shafts of wheat emblazoned on the bedspread, to the pencil post bed entwined with grape vines, our fall room delights in the riches of the earth. . . Quiet snowfalls and thoughts of Hemingway's Nick Adams stories are ideal companions for the room's gracefully hued furnishings."

Popovers with Strawberries Romanoff

Popovers, called Yorkshire pudding by the British, are glamorized by this inn's addition of Romanoff sauce. "It serves as our bread and fruit dish breakfast opener," says innkeeper Libby Johnston.

- 1 cup all-purpose flour
- 1/4 teaspoon salt
- 2 eggs
- 1 cup milk
- 1 tablespoon butter, melted
- Strawberries Romanoff as an accompaniment (recipe next page)

Preheat the oven to 425°.

Coat eight 5-ounce oven-proof custard cups with non-stick spray and place them on a large baking sheet.

In a large bowl, sift together the flour and salt. In a medium bowl, beat together the eggs, milk, and butter and gradually add this mixture to the flour, beating until it is smooth. Pour the batter into the custard cups, filling them about 1/3 full. Bake for 30 to 35 minutes, then turn off the oven. Leave the popovers in the oven until they are cooled so that they don't fall, but watch that they don't get too brown. Place each popover on a large plate and serve with Strawberries Romanoff (recipe on page 72).

Yield: 8 servings.

continued on next page

STRAWBERRIES ROMANOFF

This is best made a day ahead.

- 1 1/2 cups sour cream
- 2 tablespoons confectioners' sugar
- 1 tablespoon dark rum
- 1 teaspoon cinnamon
- 3/4 teaspoon brown sugar
- 3/4 teaspoon grated orange rind
- 16 to 24 large fresh strawberries

Combine all ingredients except strawberries, mixing well. To serve, place 2 to 3 large fresh strawberries on the plate, covering the berries with sauce. If separation occurs, just stir.

Yield: 8 servings.

BLUEBERRY STREUSEL MUFFINS

Ordinary blueberry muffins never had it so good as with the addition of this lacy streusel topping.

- 1 1/2 cups unbleached, all-purpose flour
- 1/2 cup light brown sugar, firmly packed
- 1/3 cup sugar
- 2 teaspoons baking powder
- 1 1/2 teaspoons cinnamon
- 1 tablespoon grated lemon peel
- 1/4 teaspoon salt
- 1/2 cup milk
- 1/2 cup unsalted butter, melted and cooled
- 1 egg, lightly beaten
- 3/4 cup fresh blueberries

Streusel Topping

- 1/4 cup light brown sugar, firmly packed
- 2 tablespoons unbleached, all-purpose flour
- 1 tablespoon grated lemon peel
- 2 tablespoons chopped toasted pecans
- 1 tablespoon unsalted butter, melted and cooled

Preheat the oven to 350°.

Combine the flour, sugars, baking powder, cinnamon, lemon peel and salt in a large bowl. Make a well in the center, pour the milk, butter, and egg into the center and mix until smooth. Fold in the blueberries. Spoon the batter into 12 muffin cups coated with non-stick spray, filling the cups 2/3 full.

Mix together the streusel topping ingredients in a small bowl, and top each muffin with 1 tablespoon of the mixture. Bake for 20 to 25 minutes or until a tester comes out clean. Cool the muffins for five minutes in the tin on a rack, then remove from the tin. Serve the muffins warm or at room temperature.

Yield: 12 muffins.

Broiled Tomatoes au Gratin

The inn serves these with eggs, for guests who want traditional fare with a twist.

1/2	pound bacon
1	medium onion, chopped (about 1 cup)
1/4	pound grated Swiss cheese
1/4	cup freshly minced parsley
1	tablespoon freshly chopped basil
3	large tomatoes, cut into 1/2-inch thick slices
	freshly ground pepper

In a large skillet, cook the bacon until slightly crisp, then remove to drain. Remove all but 2 tablespoons of the drippings, and sauté the onions in the skillet until they are very soft but not browned. Transfer the onions to a medium bowl and crumble in the bacon. Mix in the cheese, parsley, and basil. (The recipe can be prepared one day ahead to this point and refrigerated.)

Preheat the broiler. Arrange the tomatoes on an oiled broiler pan and season them with pepper. Top each tomato slice with some of the bacon mixture and broil the slices just until the cheese melts. (Be careful not to burn.) Serve hot.

Yield: 8 servings.

School House Bed and Breakfast

ROCHEPORT, MISSOURI

If there's one thing you can still learn at this school house turned inn, it's that you CAN get away from the busy world and relax. Decor and furnishings are simple and include reminders of school days such as the blackboard in the parlor upon which innkeepers John and Vicki Ott welcome guests by name. Rocheport is an 8-block town that's coming to life again, largely thanks to the Otts, who have restored several of its historic buildings. Rails and ties from a former railroad line were recently pulled up, making way for a bike trail that goes through Rocheport and continues for some 36 miles. Great for working off the Otts' breakfasts!

Apple Oat Bran Muffins

These muffins are even tastier with homemade apple butter.

- 1 1/4 cups all-purpose flour
- 1/2 cup sugar
- 1 tablespoon baking powder
- 1/2 teaspoon salt
- 1/2 teaspoon cinnamon
- 1/4 teaspoon nutmeg
- 1 cup oat bran
- 1 cup oat flake cereal
- 1 1/4 cups milk
- 1 egg, slightly beaten
- 1/4 cup vegetable oil
- 1/2 teaspoon vanilla extract
- 1 cup cored and chopped red baking apples
- homemade apple butter as an accompaniment, if desired.

Preheat the oven to 425°.

Mix together the first 6 ingredients in a bowl and set aside. Combine the milk, egg, oil and vanilla in a large bowl. Add the dry ingredients and apples and mix together quickly. Fill greased muffin tins 1/3 full and bake the muffins for 13-16 minutes or until they are golden.

Yield: 12 to 16 muffins.

School House Bed and Breakfast

ROCHEPORT, MISSOURI

Sausage and Mushroom Crouton Casserole

This hearty casserole warmed up my winter morning at the inn.

2	cups seasoned croutons
1	pound bulk sausage
1/4	cup parmesan cheese
1	tablespoon Mrs. Dash™ or seasoning of choice
4	eggs, slightly beaten
3	cups milk
1	can condensed cream of mushroom soup
1	teaspoon dried mustard
1	cup shredded Cheddar cheese

Coat a 9 x 13-inch baking pan with non-stick spray and spread the croutons over the bottom. Brown the sausage in a large skillet over medium heat and drain. Spread the sausage over the croutons, and sprinkle with the parmesan cheese and seasoning. Mix together the eggs, milk, soup, and dried mustard and pour the mixture over the sausage and croutons. Cover the casserole and refrigerate it overnight.

The next morning, let the casserole stand at room temperature for 30 minutes and preheat the oven to 325°. Bake the casserole for 1 hour or until it is lightly browned. Remove the casserole from the oven and sprinkle the Cheddar cheese over the top, then cover it with aluminum foil and let it stand for 15 minutes before serving.

Yield: 8 to 10 servings.

Coachlight Bed and Breakfast

ST. LOUIS, MISSOURI

Susan and Chuck Sundermeyer's three-room B&B, in busy St. Louis, is an elegant but soothing and comfortable respite decorated with soft fabrics and easy colors. Business travelers flock here. Coachlight is in a historic neighborhood within walking distance of boutiques, galleries, and restaurants.

Poppy Colada Muffins

An unusual mix that originated with Susan's mother.

- 1 package (18 1/4 ounces) white cake mix
- 1 package (3 3/4 ounces) instant coconut pudding mix
- 1 carton (6 ounces) piña colada yogurt
- 2 eggs
- 1 cup hot water
- 1/2 cup vegetable oil
- 1/4 cup poppy seed

Preheat the oven to 350°.

In a large mixing bowl, beat all ingredients together by hand until they are well mixed. Pour the batter into 18 greased and floured muffin cups. Bake the muffins for 20 to 30 minutes, until a tester comes out clean. Do not brown.

Yield: 18 muffins.

Coachlight Bed and Breakfast

ST. LOUIS, MISSOURI

Vegetable Breakfast Quiche

One way to ensure getting your daily dose of five fruits and vegetables is to eat three of them for breakfast in this vegetarian staple.

1	tablespoon vegetable oil
1	cup chopped onion
1/4	cup diced carrot
1/2	cup small broccoli florets
1/2	cup chopped ham
1	cup shredded cheddar cheese
4	eggs
2 1/2	tablespoons butter, melted
1/2	cup flour
1/2	cup Cheddar cheese, shredded

Preheat the oven to 350°.

Heat the oil in a medium skillet and sauté the onions in the oil over low heat until they are soft but not brown. Set aside. In a steamer set over boiling water, steam the carrots for 8 to 10 minutes, or until tender. Remove the carrots and in the same steamer, cook the broccoli for 5 to 7 minutes, or until tender. Mix the onion, vegetables, ham and 1/2 cup of the cheese and spread in an oiled 8" quiche dish. In a blender, mix together the eggs, butter, and flour. Pour the mixture over the vegetables and sprinkle the remaining cheese over the top. Bake the quiche for 40 minutes or until it is set.

Yield: 6 servings.

Coachlight Bed and Breakfast

ST. LOUIS, MISSOURI

FRUITED PECAN SAUCE

Try this interesting sauce instead of maple syrup on pancakes, waffles or French toast.

- 1/3 cup butter
- 2/3 cup brown sugar
- 3 tablespoons orange juice
- 1 cup sliced fresh strawberries
- 1 cup sliced bananas
- 1/4 cup sliced kiwi
- 1/4 cup pecans, toasted

Melt the butter in a medium saucepan. Stir in the sugar and the orange juice and add the fruits and nuts. Heat the sauce slowly but do not boil. Serve hot.

Yield: 1 cup.

Lafayette House

ST. LOUIS, MISSOURI

Sarah Milligan is one of those innkeepers who genuinely treats all who enter her urban inn as family. Guests are free to meander through piles of the latest blockbuster novels or research books; magazines are everywhere, as are many of Sarah's accumulated collections of a lifetime. Sarah is also a successful teacher of innkeeping. Her husband Jack is a cartographer by day and a host with a plethora of interesting facts by night.

Peanut Butter Bread

No matter what your age, this is one bread that will delight all your senses.

- 2 cups all-purpose flour
- 2 teaspoons baking powder
- 1/2 teaspoon salt
- 1/2 cup sugar
- 3 1/2 tablespoons shortening
- 1 jar (6 1/2 ounces) peanut butter, smooth or chunky
- 2 eggs, beaten
- 1 cup milk

Preheat the oven to 325°.

Sift together the flour, baking powder, salt, and sugar in a bowl. Cut in the shortening and peanut butter, using an electric mixer. Mix well. Combine the eggs and milk, add to the flour mixture and blend well. Bake in a greased 8 x 4 x 2-inch baking pan for 1 1/4 hours or until a tester comes out clean.

Yield: 1 loaf.

Orange Marmalade Bread

The marmalade gives this bread a refreshing flavor and a moist texture.

1	egg, beaten
4	tablespoons butter, melted and cooled
1	jar (16 ounces) orange marmalade
3/4	cup orange juice
3	cups all-purpose flour
3	teaspoons baking powder
1	teaspoon baking soda
1/4	teaspoon salt
1	cup chopped pecans

Preheat the oven to 350°.

Mix together the egg and butter, all but 1/4 cup of the marmalade and the orange juice. Sift together the flour, baking powder, baking soda, and salt and add to the egg mixture along with the nuts.

Pour the batter into a greased 9 x 5-inch loaf pan. Bake for 1 hour, or until a tester comes out clean. Remove the bread from the oven and turn out of the pan onto a baking sheet. Spread the reserved marmalade over the top. Return the bread to the oven for 2 minutes or until the marmalade glazes. Cool the bread before cutting.

Yield: 1 loaf.

The Inn at Honey Run

MILLERSBURG, OHIO

Some of the guest rooms at the inn are literally tucked into a ridge—sort of a big berm—with picture window views of a fabulous countryside. Each has a wood-burning fireplace and whirlpool bath. Shaker and Early American furnishings blend easily with a contemporary setting. Innkeeper Marge Stock is always on hand, heading a largely Amish staff.

Honey Run Sticky Buns

Marge had young children test this recipe for her. If they can do it, so can you.

- 1/4 cup sugar
- 1/2 teaspoon salt
- 1 package (1/4 ounce) active dry yeast
- 2 1/2 to 3 1/4 cups all-purpose flour
- 1 cup milk
- 1/4 cup butter
- 1 egg

Filling

- 1/4 cup butter, melted
- 1/3 cup sugar
- 2 teaspoons cinnamon

Topping

- 1/3 cup butter
- 1/2 cup light brown sugar, packed
- 2 teaspoons light corn syrup

In a large bowl, combine the 1/4 cup sugar, salt, and yeast and 1 1/4 cups of the flour. In a small saucepan, over low heat, slowly heat the milk and the 1/4 cup butter until very warm (120° to 130°). With an electric mixer set at low speed, gradually add the liquid to the dry ingredients. Increase the speed, beating 3 minutes more. Beat in the egg and 1/2 cup flour and continue beating for 2 minutes. Stir in additional flour to make a soft dough.

Turn the dough onto a lightly floured surface and knead until it is smooth and elastic, about 10 minutes. Shape the dough into a ball, place it in a greased bowl, cover and let rise in a warm place until double in bulk, about 1 hour. Punch the dough down, and on a lightly floured surface, roll it into a 9 x 24-inch rectangle.

continued on next page

Honey Run Sticky Buns (continued)

For the filling, brush the dough with the melted butter. Combine the 1/3 cup sugar and the cinnamon and sprinkle over the dough. Roll up the dough jelly roll style, starting at the widest end. Seal the seam. Cut the roll crosswise into 24 slices.

To make the topping, combine the 1/3 cup butter, brown sugar, and corn syrup in a small saucepan. Cook over low heat, stirring occasionally, until the sugar is dissolved. Bring the mixture to a boil, stirring constantly. Remove from the heat. Continue stirring until the mixture is smooth, and pour the topping immediately into 2 greased 9 x 13-inch baking pans, spreading it evenly over the bottoms. Place the dough slices on top of the topping in the baking pans. Cover the buns and let them rise in a warm place until doubled in size, about 30 minutes.

Preheat the oven to 400°. Bake the sticky buns for 12 to 15 minutes or until they are lightly browned. Remove the pans from oven and immediately loosen the sides of the buns with a spatula. Invert the pans onto cookie sheets covered with aluminum foil. Serve warm.

Yield: 24 buns.

The Wisconsin House Stage Coach Inn

HAZEL GREEN, WISCONSIN

It looked like a stagecoach stop some 150 years ago, and it still looks that way today. However, travelers finding their way to John and Betha Mueller's place find much more than a mere stopover. Guests can walk up or down the same staircase Ulysses S. Grant used during the 1860s. Early American and Scandinavian furnishings are scattered about the inn. And the innkeepers have been known to perform a polka for guests after meal time!

Swedish Almond Twists

Betha says she makes dozens of these at the inn. They usually make the rounds at the breakfast table twice.

- 1 package (1/4 ounce) cake or active dry yeast
- 1/4 cup warm water
- 1 cup milk
- 2/3 cup sugar
- 1/2 cup butter
- 1 teaspoon salt
- 3 eggs, beaten
- 5 1/2 cups all-purpose flour

Filling

- 4 tablespoons butter, melted
- 1/3 cup sugar
- 1/2 cup ground almonds
- 3 tablespoons sugar

Almond Glaze

- 1 cup confectioners' sugar
- 1 to 2 tablespoons milk
- 1/4 teaspoon almond extract

Dissolve the yeast in the warm water. Heat the milk to boiling, remove from the heat, and stir in the 2/3 cup sugar, 1/2 cup butter, and the salt. Cool the mixture for 20 minutes to lukewarm (105° to 115°) and stir in the yeast. In a mixing bowl, combine the milk mixture, eggs, and flour, adding up to 1/2 cup additional flour if needed. Form a smooth dough and knead for 3 to 5 minutes on a floured surface until dough is moderately soft. Place the dough in a greased bowl, cover and let rise until doubled in size (about 1 1/4 to 1 1/2 hours).

continued on next page

The Wisconsin House Stage Coach Inn

HAZEL GREEN, WISCONSIN

Swedish Almond Twists (continued)

Punch the dough down and divide it into 2 equal portions. Cover the dough pieces and let them rest for 10 minutes. Roll out 1 portion into a 12 by 14-inch rectangle. Spread with half the melted butter, half the 1/3 cup sugar, and half the almonds. Starting with the short end, roll up the dough jelly roll fashion and seal the seam. Cut the roll crosswise into 12 pieces. Stretch each piece to a 4 to 5-inch length, twist, and place on a greased baking sheet, pressing the ends down. Repeat this process with the remaining dough. Sprinkle the twists with the 3 tablespoons sugar.

Let the bread rise in a warm place until almost doubled (about 50 to 60 minutes).

Mix the ingredients for the almond glaze together in a small bowl and set aside. Bake the twists in a preheated 375° oven for 12 to 15 minutes. Let them cool slightly on wire racks, then drizzle with the glaze.

Yield: 24 twists.

West

Prescott Pines

PRESCOTT, ARIZONA

Breakfast is served in front of a rolling fire on winter mornings, as guests gather around two oak tables to enjoy the hospitality of innkeepers Jean Wu and Michael Acton. The main house has four guest rooms, two other houses have seven rooms, and in addition there is a large chalet for families. The 1902 inn is surrounded by Ponderosa plant life.

Berry Power Drink

Serve this as a prelude to a light breakfast or make it your breakfast in a glass. For the smoothest drink, process for the full time.

- 1 cup cranberry or pineapple juice
- 1 cup fresh or frozen strawberries
- 8 ounces vanilla lowfat yogurt
- 2/3 cup uncooked quick oats
- 1 cup ice cubes

Place all the ingredients except for the ice cubes in a blender. Whirl on high 2 minutes or until smooth. Gradually add the ice and whirl another minute or two.

Yield: Two 10-ounce servings.

Lemon Yogurt Pancakes

Jean's pancakes are incredibly light and fluffy. They are a pleasure to make and serve. Feel free to experiment with different flavored yogurts, omitting the lemon peel.

1	large egg
1/2	cup lemon yogurt
1/2	cup milk
2	tablespoons vegtable oil
1	tablespoon sugar
1/2	teaspoon grated lemon peel
1/8	teaspoon nutmeg
1	cup unbleached all-purpose flour
1	teaspoon baking powder
1/2	teaspoon baking soda
	butter and maple syrup for serving

In a medium bowl, beat the egg and mix in the yogurt, milk, and oil. Stir in the sugar, lemon peel, and nutmeg. Sift together the flour, baking powder and baking soda in a separate bowl. Add the flour mixture to the liquid and mix well. The batter will be a bit thick.

Lightly grease a griddle and heat it to medium high. For each pancake, pour 1/4 cup batter onto the griddle. Cook the pancakes until they are puffed and turn them to finish cooking. Serve with butter and maple syrup.

Yield: 8 pancakes.

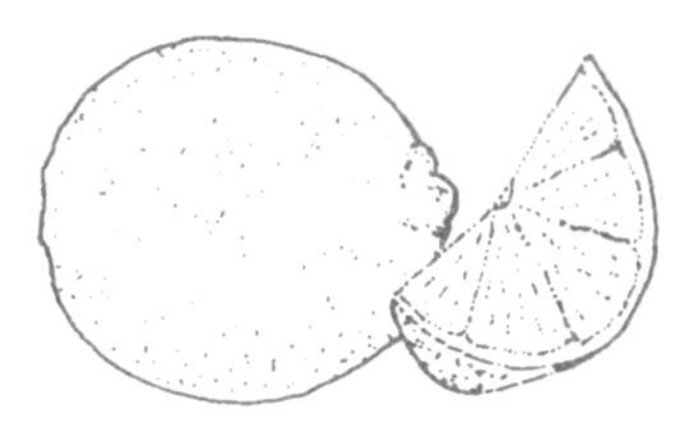

Cheese-Filled Poppy Seed Muffins

These can be made ahead, wrapped and stored in the freezer. Warm them in the microwave on high for a minute to reheat.

- 1 1/4 cups quick oats
- 1 1/2 cups all-purpose flour
- 1/3 cup sugar
- 3/4 cup chopped dried apples or raisins
- 1 tablespoon baking powder
- 1 cup milk
- 3 tablespoons corn oil
- 2 egg whites, beaten slightly

Filling

- 3/4 cup skim milk Ricotta cheese
- 1 egg white, beaten slightly
- 4 teaspoons sugar

Preheat the oven to 375°.

In a large bowl, mix together the oats, flour, sugar, fruit and baking powder. Add the milk, oil, and egg whites to the fruit mixture and mix just until moistened. Combine the filling ingredients in a separate bowl.

Spoon 1 tablespoon batter into each of 12 paper-lined muffin cups and follow with 1 tablespoon of the cheese filling. Finish by spreading additional batter evenly into each cup. Bake the muffins for 20 to 25 minutes or until they are lightly browned.

Yield: 12 muffins.

The Goose and Turrets

MONTARA, CALIFORNIA

Breakfast is an abundant four-course delight here. Fog horns sound off the peninsula and there are down comforters everywhere. The inn is housed in a 1908 Italian villa in a quiet seaside village of horse ranches and strawflower farms. At breakfast, innkeepers Emily and Raymond Hoche-Mong play the music of trumpets and Australian bird calls. They have a great outlook at this friendly and educationally stimulating inn.

Strawberry Orange Drink

Easy to make and looks like an ice cream soda. The orange flower water in the recipe is used prolifically in the Middle East for whatever ails you. Here, it's available in gourmet shops and is used as a flavoring.

- 1 1/2 pounds fresh strawberries, cleaned, hulled, and halved
- 1/2 cup sugar
- 1/4 cup lime juice
- 1/4 teaspoon orange flower water
- 1/2 ounce Cointreau liqueur
- 1/4 cup simple syrup (Bring 1/4 cup sugar and 1/4 cup water to a boil. You will have a little left over.)
- 2 cups chilled orange juice
- whipped cream, for garnish
- mint leaves, for garnish

Toss the berries with the sugar and allow them to macerate overnight in the refrigerator. The next morning, purée the berries in a blender, adding the lime juice, orange flower water, Cointreau, simple syrup and 1/2 cup of the orange juice. Pour the mixture into a large pitcher, add the remaining orange juice and stir. Taste, and add more simple syrup for a sweeter drink. Serve the drink in individual parfait glasses with iced tea spoons, garnished with a dollop of whipped cream and a sprig of mint.

Yield: 8 to 10 servings.

Chilled Champagne Honeydew Soup

This chilled soup would be impressive for any breakfast.

- 3 ripe honeydew melons, seeded and rind removed
- juice from 3 freshly squeezed oranges (about 1 1/4 cups)
- juice from 3 freshly squeezed limes (about 1/3 cup)
- 3 tablespoons honey
- 1 cup champagne
- 1/2 cup heavy cream, whipped
- peppermint leaves, as a garnish
- slices of kiwi fruit, as a garnish
- nasturtium petals, as a garnish

Purée melons in batches, using a food processor. Transfer to a bowl and stir in juices and honey. Refrigerate the soup overnight. Stir in the champagne and serve in chilled bowls (crystal would be nice!). Garnish each serving with a dollop of whipped cream, a peppermint leaf, a slice of kiwi, and a nasturtium petal.

Yield: 8 to 10 servings.

The Goose and Turrets

MONTARA, CALIFORNIA

Egyptian Bean Breakfast (Foul Madamas)

Serve this with pita bread and "instruct your family to mash the whole thing up together and eat hearty," explains Emily. Raymond developed this recipe after years of living in Cairo. He suggests serving it as the cereal course. This recipe is for one serving — expand it as you like.

- 1/4 cup dried fava beans
- pinch baking soda
- 1/4 teaspoon salt
- 1 hard-boiled egg, whole (optional)
- 1 tablespoon chopped onion
- 1 tablespoon cardamom
- 1 tablespoon lemon juice
- 1 tablespoon extra virgin olive oil
- 1 teaspoon cumin
- 1/4 teaspoon coarsely ground black pepper

Cover the beans with water, add the baking soda and let soak for 8 hours. Drain the beans and put them in a pressure cooker with fresh water to cover and the salt. Cook for about 20 to 30 minutes. Let the beans stay in the liquid overnight, refrigerated.

The next morning, warm the beans (be careful not to burn them). Place in a soup plate, make a well in the center and follow with the other ingredients.

Yield: 1 serving.

Seal Cove Inn

MOSS BEACH, CALIFORNIA

Karen Brown started learning the ABCs of innkeeping when she took a year off from college to travel to Europe. She wrote her first European guidebook then and started what is today a growing literary series of 14 books (Karen Brown's Country Inns), directing travelers to country inns abroad. Karen was then inspired to open her own inn with husband Rick and their two children. This author-turned-innkeeper now works with a spatula in one hand and a pen in the other.

Cheddar Sandwiches with Maple Cranberry Apricot Sauce

The contrast of Cheddar with the tanginess of the fruits and the sweetness of the maple creates a harmonious symphony of flavors.

- 20 slices sourdough bread
- 1/2 cup butter
- 1 pound sharp Cheddar cheese, thinly sliced
- 12 eggs
- 3 cups light cream or milk
- 3 tablespoons vanilla extract
- Maple Cranberry Apricot Sauce (recipe at right)

Butter half the bread slices and divide the cheese equally among the others. Pair the bread slices with the buttered sides turned in. Whisk together the eggs, cream, and vanilla until smooth. Soak the sandwiches in the egg mixture for at least 5 minutes and drain. Grill the sandwiches in a well-greased skillet over medium heat until the cheese is melted and the bread is slightly brown. Serve with Maple Cranberry Apricot Sauce.

Yield: 10 servings.

Maple Cranberry Apricot Sauce

- 1 cup pure maple syrup
- 1/4 cup dried cranberries
- 1/4 cup thinly sliced apricots (fresh or canned)
- 1/4 cup finely chopped walnuts
- 1/4 cup golden raisins

Heat all the ingredients in a deep saucepan, stirring until they are well combined.

RiverSong

ESTES PARK, COLORADO

Estes Park is literally tucked into the Rockies in a wonderfully windy, mountainous region. Here, RiverSong offers its melodious tunes of hospitality with romantic, dramatic and rustic accommodations such as Indian Paintbrush, Shooting Star, Chiming Bells, and Forget-Me-Not: rooms named after regional wildflowers. Breathtaking views are everywhere.

John Wayne Corn Cheese Casserole

Innkeeper Gary Mansfield, a Southwestern cuisine buff, suggests serving this with corn muffins and picante sauce.

- 8 large eggs, separated
- 2 tablespoons butter
- 1 large onion, chopped
- 1/4 cup chopped ham
- 1/2 cup diced green chilies from a 4-ounce can, drained well
- 1/4 cup chopped Anaheim chilies
- 1/2 cup all-purpose flour
- 2 1/4 cups sour cream
- 2 cups frozen corn kernels, thawed
- 2 cups grated mild Cheddar cheese
- 2 cups grated Monterey Jack cheese
- 1 teaspoon garlic powder

Preheat the oven to 325°.

Beat the egg whites until they begin to stiffen and set them aside. Beat the yolks and set aside. In a large skillet, melt the butter and sauté the onions, ham and chilies until the onions are slightly brown. Mix together the egg yolks, flour, sour cream, corn, cheeses, and garlic powder, and fold in the egg whites. Bake the mixture in a greased 9 x 13-inch baking pan for 45 minutes to 1 hour or until it is lightly browned.

Gloria's Spouting Horn

KAUAI, HAWAII

"Aloha" is the welcoming greeting spoken in Hawaii. I enjoyed the inviting surf that breaks 40 feet from the five guest rooms. Coconut palm trees bristle gently as you savor a tropical breakfast complete with native fruits.

Pele's Baked Pear Dumplings with Lemon Sauce

Pele is the Hawaiian goddess of fire. A volcano of striking flavors erupts from the pastry shells when you dig in.

6	small, very ripe pears with stems attached
3	tablespoons butter, softened
1/3	cup pecans, coarsely chopped
1/3	cup brown sugar
1	teaspoon cinnamon
2	packages (8 ounces each) crescent rolls, triangles separated
1	egg, beaten
	Lemon Sauce (recipe at right)
	shredded coconut and mint sprigs, for garnish

Preheat the oven to 350°.

Peel the pears, and core them from the bottom, leaving the stems intact. Mix the butter, pecans, brown sugar, and cinnamon to form a paste. Generously fill the pear cavities with the paste. Using 2 triangles of dough, cover each pear completely, except for the stems. Brush the pears with the beaten egg. Bake the dumplings for 50 minutes or until the crusts are golden brown. Ladle Lemon Sauce over each dumpling and sprinkle with coconut. Garnish with a sprig of mint.

Yield: 6 dumplings.

Lemon Sauce

1	cup water
1	cup sugar
	grated rind and juice of
1	lemon
2	egg yolks, beaten
2	tablespoons cornstarch

Combine the water, sugar, grated rind and lemon juice in a saucepan. Boil for 3 to 5 minutes and strain. Slowly stir the sauce into the egg yolks until they are well blended. Add 2 tablespoons of the lemon sauce to the corn starch and mix well. Combine this mixture with the lemon sauce in the saucepan and bring to a boil, stirring constantly until it is thick and creamy.

Yield: Approximately 1 1/4 cups.

Hawaiian Müesli

The Swiss version of müesli is moistened with milk and fresh fruit; this tropical rendering is topped with juice and yogurt.

1	cup quick oats
1/2	cup apple juice
1	can (8 ounces) crushed pineapple with juice
1	small red apple, cored
8	ounces vanilla yogurt
	additional yogurt, brown sugar and fruit, for serving

In a medium bowl, combine the oats, apple juice, and pineapple. Cover and refrigerate for several hours or overnight. Just before serving, coarsely shred the apple. Stir the apple and yogurt into the müesli. To serve, top with additional yogurt, brown sugar, and papaya, mango, banana, berries, or melon.

Yield: 4 servings.

CRAB AND PASTA FRITTATA

The pasta ensures a nourishing day-opener and the seafood has fewer calories than some breakfast meats.

- 1/2 pound thin spaghetti
- 2 to 3 tablespoons butter
- 1/3 cup chopped onion
- 1/3 cup chopped green, red and yellow pepper
- 1/3 cup shredded zucchini
- 6 eggs, beaten
- 1/3 cup grated Parmesan cheese
- 1/2 cup grated provolone cheese
- 1/2 cup flaked crabmeat

Preheat oven to 350°.

Cook the spaghetti for 8 to 10 minutes in boiling salted water. Meanwhile, melt the butter in a skillet and sauté the vegetables until they are tender, but not browned. When the spaghetti is cooked, drain it, run cold water over it, and drain it again. Mix the spaghetti with the eggs and add the vegetables, cheeses and crabmeat, combining well. Pour the mixture into a greased 9 x 13-inch casserole. Bake, covered with foil, for 25-30 minutes, or until the mixture turns slightly golden.

Yield: 8 servings.

Cowslip's Belle

ASHLAND, OREGON

"All the world's a stage," wrote William Shakespeare. Cowslip's Belle, a name from one of the writer's great plays, is located only three blocks from Shakespearean theaters and festivals. So it's curtain call at the inn each morning when Jon and Carmen Reinhardt serve their tasty eye-openers. Can you guess which play cowslip's comes from? Hint: It's not a name associated with winter.

Crunchy French Toast with Strawberry Cream Sauce

The melangé of sweet fruit, sour cream and cereal creates a heavenly-hash of French toasts.

- 1 cup evaporated milk
- 2 large eggs
- 3 tablespoons water
- 2 tablespoons sugar
- 1 tablespoon vanilla extract
- 1 teaspoon cinnamon
- 8 slices (about 1 inch thick) French bread
- 2 cups crushed corn or oat flake cereal or granola
- confectioners' sugar
- Strawberry Cream Sauce (recipe at right)
- 1/2 pint fresh strawberries, sliced, for garnish

In a medium bowl, combine the first six ingredients. Dip the bread slices into the mixture and then coat each slice with cereal. Heat a buttered skillet and cook each piece until golden and crisp. To serve, place two pieces of toast on each plate and sprinkle lightly with confectioners sugar. Garnish with Strawberry Cream Sauce and strawberries.

Yield: 4 servings.

Strawberry Cream Sauce

- 1 package (10 ounces) frozen sweetened strawberries, thawed
- 1 cup sour cream or plain yogurt
- 1/2 teaspoon cinnamon

Mix the strawberries with the sour cream and add the cinnamon.

Yield: Approximately 2 cups.

THREE CHEESE CROISSANTS

This recipe gives an eye-appealing twist to the crescent-shaped rolls.

4	large croissants, split into top and bottom halves
2	cups grated Swiss cheese
1/4	cup grated Parmesan
1/4	cup grated Monterey Jack or mozzarella cheese
5	large eggs
1	cup skim milk
1/2	teaspoon pepper
1/8	teaspoon nutmeg
1/8	teaspoon salt, if desired

Preheat the oven to 350°.

Butter 4 au gratin dishes. Place the bottom half of each croissant in a dish, cut side up. Spread Swiss cheese on each, saving about 1/2 cup to sprinkle on top. Follow with all of the Parmesan and Monterey Jack, dividing each cheese equally among the croissants. In a medium bowl, beat the eggs, milk, and seasonings until they are frothy. Pour 2/3 cup of the egg mixture over each croissant and replace the tops. Sprinkle the remaining Swiss cheese evenly over the tops. Bake 20 minutes or until the eggs are set and the croissants are a golden brown.

Yield: 4 servings.

The Captain Whidbey Inn

COUPEVILLE, WASHINGTON

If it's nautical atmosphere you're after, The Captain Whidbey is the most seafaring of country inns. Innkeeper John Colby Stone is at the helm of his 1907 house, "steering" this divine get-away overlooking a cove and lagoon.

Crabmeat Eggs in Creole Hollandaise

- 2 eggs
- 1 tablespoon vinegar
- 1 English muffin, split in half
- 1 tablespoon butter
- 2 ounces snow crabmeat
- Creole Hollandaise Sauce (recipe at right)

Poach eggs for 3 to 4 minutes in simmering water to which the vinegar has been added. Toast the English muffin halves. Melt the butter in a small skillet and heat the crabmeat gently for 1 to 2 minutes. When the eggs are just set, remove them from the pan with a slotted spoon and drain them on paper towels. Place one egg on top of each muffin half. Cover each egg with crabmeat and 1/4 cup of Creole Hollandaise Sauce.

Yield: 2 servings.

Creole Hollandaise Sauce

- 6 egg yolks
- 3/4 cup butter, clarified
- 2 tablespoons hot pepper sauce
- 2 green onions, minced
- juice of 1/4 lemon
- salt and white pepper to taste
- 1/2 teaspoon cayenne pepper

Beat the egg yolks over simmering water until they are thick, and remove them from the heat. Add the clarified butter in a stream, beating constantly. Add the remaining ingredients and stir. Serve warm.

Note: For clarified butter, let the butter stand after melting and use only the clear liquid which separates from the milky solids.

Inn Directory

Inn Directory

Arizona

Prescott Pines Inn
901 White Spar Road
(Highway 89 South)
Prescott, AZ 86303
(602) 445-7270
(800) 541-5374 (reservations/brochure)

California

The Goose and Turrets Bed and Breakfast
835 George Street
Montara, CA 94037
(415) 728-5451

Seal Cove Inn
221 Cypress Avenue
Moss Beach, CA 94038
(415) 728-7325

Colorado

RiverSong Bed and Breakfast Inn
P.O. Box 1910
Estes Park, CO 80517
(303) 586-4666

Connecticut

Manor House
P.O. Box 447
69 Maple Avenue
Norfolk, CT 06058
(203) 542-5690

Florida

Florida House Inn
P.O. Box 688
Amelia Island, FL 32034
(904) 261-3300
(800) 258-3301 (reservations)

Georgia

The Gastonian
220 East Gaston Street
Savannah, GA 31401
(912) 232-2869

Hawaii

Gloria's Spouting Horn
4464 Lawai Beach Road
Poipu, Kauai, Hawaii 96756
(808) 742-6995

Illinois

Maple Leaf Cottage Inn
12 Selma/P.O. Box 156
Historic Elsah, IL 62028
(618) 374-1684

Sweet Basil Hill Farm
15937 W. Washington Street
Gurnee, IL 60031
(708) 244-3333
(800) 228-HERB (reservations)

Iowa

The Redstone Inn
504 Bluff Street
Dubuque, IA 52001
(319) 582-1894

Maine

The Cape Neddick House
Route 1, P.O. Box 70
Cape Neddick, ME 03902
(207) 363-2500

Massachusetts

The Gables Inn
103 Walker Street
Route 183
Lenox, MA 01240
(413) 637-3416

Michigan

The Inn at Union Pier
P.O. Box 222
9708 Berrien Street
Union Pier, MI 49129
(616) 469-4700

Victorian Villa
601 N. Broadway Street
Union City, MI 49094
(517) 741-7383

Missouri

Coachlight Bed and Breakfast
P.O. Box 8095
St. Louis, MO 63156
(314) 367-5870

Lafayette House
2156 Lafayette Avenue
St. Louis, MO 63104
(314) 772-4429

School House Bed and Breakfast
Third and Clark Streets
Rocheport, MO 65279
(314) 698-2022

New Jersey

The Cabbage Rose Inn
162 Main Street
Flemington, NJ 08822
(908) 788-0247

The Queen Victoria
102 Ocean Street
Cape May, NJ 08204
(609) 884-8702

New York

Blushing Rose Bed and Breakfast
11 William Street
Hammondsport, NY 14840
(607) 569-3402

The Village Victorian Inn at Rhinebeck
31 Center Street
Rhinebeck, NY 12572
(914) 876-8345

North Carolina

The Lodge on Lake Lure
Route One, Box 529-A
Lake Lure, NC 28746
(704) 625-2789

The Mast Farm Inn
P.O. Box 704
Valle Crucis, NC 28691
(704) 963-5857

Ohio

The Inn at Honey Run
6920 County Road 203
Millersburg, OH 44654
(216) 674-0011
(800) 468-6639 (Ohio only)

Oregon

Cowslip's Belle
159 N. Main Street
Ashland, OR 97520
(503) 488-2901

Pennsylvania

Goose Chase
200 Blueberry Road
Gardners, PA 17324
(717) 528-8877

Swiss Woods Bed and Breakfast
500 Blantz Road
Lititz, PA 17543
(717) 627-3358
(800) 594-8018 (reservations)

The Whitehall Inn
RD 2, Box 250
Pineville Road
New Hope, PA 18938
(215) 598-7945

Tennessee

Edgeworth Inn
P.O. Box 340
Monteagle, TN 37356
(615) 924-2669

Texas

McKay House Bed and Breakfast
306 E. Delta Street
Jefferson, TX 75657
(903) 665-7322 (Jefferson)
(214) 348-1929 (Dallas)

Vermont

Cornucopia of Dorset
Route 30
P.O. Box 307
Dorset, VT 05251
(802) 867-5751

The Governor's Inn
86 Main Street
Ludlow, VT 05149
(802) 228-8830

Windham Hill Inn
West Townshend, VT 05359
(802) 874-4080

Virginia

Newport House Bed and Breakfast
710 S. Henry Street
Williamsburg, VA 23185
(804) 229-1775

The Shadows Bed and Breakfast Inn
14294 Constitution Highway
Route 1, Box 535
Orange, VA 22960
(703) 672-5057

Washington

The Captain Whidbey Inn
2072 W. Captain Whidbey Inn Road
Coupeville, WA 98239
(206) 678-4097

Wisconsin

Wisconsin House Stage Coach Inn
2105 East Main
Hazel Green, WI 53811
(608) 854-2233

Menus

Use the following space to create your own menus or to make notes about which dishes were served to guests.

DATE: ______________________________

GUESTS: ______________________________

MENU: ______________________________

____

____

DATE: ______________________________

GUESTS: ______________________________

MENU: ______________________________

____

____

DATE: ______________________________

GUESTS: ______________________________

MENU: ______________________________

____

____

DATE: ______________________________

GUESTS: ______________________________

MENU: ______________________________

____

____

Cook's Notes

Use the following space to make notes about the recipes you prepare from this book. Record any variations or subsitutions from the recipe, special pans or equipment used, side dishes or accompaniments, cooking times, etc.

RECIPE: ______________________________

COMMENTS: ______________________________

____

____

____

RECIPE: ______________________________

COMMENTS: ______________________________

____

____

____

RECIPE: ______________________________

COMMENTS: ______________________________

____

____

____

RECIPE: ______________________________

COMMENTS: ______________________________

____

____

____

Cook's Notes

RECIPE: ______________________________

COMMENTS: ______________________________

____

____

____

RECIPE: ______________________________

COMMENTS: ______________________________

____

____

____

RECIPE: ______________________________

COMMENTS: ______________________________

____

____

____

RECIPE: ______________________________

COMMENTS: ______________________________

____

____

____

Travel Notes

I hope you can personally visit the many wonderful inns listed in this book. Make note of when and where you stayed and how you liked the food and atmosphere. These notes will be useful for future trips or when making recommendations.

INN: ____________________

COMMENTS: ____________________

INN: ____________________

COMMENTS: ____________________

INN: ____________________

COMMENTS: ____________________

INN: ____________________

COMMENTS: ____________________